EAT MORE GREEK

CONOR CURRAN

Everyday recipes for the time you have

murdoch books
Sydney | London

CONTENTS

INTRODUCTION

Hi, I'm Conor. I'm so glad you're here and getting stuck into my cookbook, *Eat More Greek*. It's built around three very simple words.

APPROACHABLE

AFFORDABLE

ACHIEVABLE

That's what I kept in my mind the whole time I was writing these recipes, and they're why this isn't, and will never be, a classic Greek cookbook. The recipes will venture from deeply entrenched in history with no changes, to a couple of switches, to just inspiration and everything in between. Because yes, I am Greek and my cooking journey was brought to me via my yiayia and eating Greek food, but I am also a person who lives in Melbourne, Australia. Someone who has travelled the world, lived in London and eaten from every cuisine imaginable. Someone who doesn't live in Greece and who has access to ingredients stocked in markets or supermarkets.

That last part is very important to me: that the everyday person can access the ingredients. A qualm of mine with Greek cookbooks over the years has been that they stick to traditional ingredients with very little wiggle room. I didn't want this book to be hard to cook from. I am not expecting any of you to head to a Mediterranean deli an hour's drive across town, so a lot of the recipes have swaps or use more readily available ingredients, like my Wilted weeds recipe (page 118), which features spinach rather than sourcing wild Grecian weeds – something that is borderline impossible.

Also important to me is that you can feel comfortable giving these recipes a go, and it helps to know how much time you'll need to achieve each one. So, I have divided them into chapters depending on how long they'll take to make from start to finish. There are plenty of 30-minute dishes (page 27) you can cook when you're up against it, designed for weeknights. Got an hour or a couple, or even a lazy Sunday spare? There are chapters for each of these timeframes too (turn to page 87, 135 and 183, respectively). And for the recipes that need overnight – be it marinating, setting, pickling, draining – to become something truly magical (minus much work from you), the 'I've got overnight' chapter (page 207) is the place to head.

These recipes are ones I love, ones I cook all the time, some I cook for special occasions and ones I have eaten at tavernas in Greece, but one thing remains true for all of them: every recipe must be delicious. Delicious isn't achieved through buying truffles and high-quality olive oil. It can be achieved with incredibly affordable and simple ingredients cooked in a way that makes magic. That's what Greek food is at its heart: simple ingredients cooked with love and flavours that just make your heart warm.

Greek food hasn't had the marketing campaign Italian food has had over the years. Most people know how to put together a pasta or a parmigiana, and Italian cuisine has engraved itself in our everyday eating and on restaurant menus. I want the same for Greek food. I guess you could call it my food mission, but if this book helps make your kitchen a little bit more Greek, I will be over the moon. The easy way we can put together a weeknight pasta is how I would love to see people putting together my Garlic and tomato pasta (page 61) or spending a Sunday making my family's Meat pasta bake (page 189). All the dishes in this book have a familiarity, and have been written in a way to make sure you succeed. Some are trickier than others, but the majority of recipes I think most of you will knock out of the park. Very importantly though, the key to being a really good cook is making mistakes and going again.

I want this book to do a lot of things for you reading it at home. I want it to turn your kitchen a little bit more Greek. I want it to get messy from the splatters of tomato-based sauces hitting the page. I want it to introduce you to Greek ingredients in a gentle way. I want it to be something to flick through for inspiration. I even want it to look good on your coffee table. But more than anything I want it to help you, my lovely reader, eat more Greek.

All my love,

Conor, @creamy_confusion

I PROMISE YOU, I'M GREEK

Conor Michael Curran. My name doesn't scream Hellenic connection, it doesn't implore you, dear reader, or anyone else to trust me in my Greek cooking. So let me unpack it, and maybe put your mind at ease that I am someone who, despite growing up in Australia, has always been in a very Greek bubble. My baba, or father, is Irish Australian and is many generations in from when that side of the family arrived in Australia and settled in the country town of Mildura, where Baba grew up. He would travel through many country towns as my pop would move jobs for his work. Baba came to Melbourne as a teenager and worked his way up in the transport logistics industry. My dad's name is Michael Curran.

Along his journey, he met my mum, who is a first-generation Greek Australian. The eldest of three girls, she grew up in a house in Clifton Hill, Melbourne, with a gloriously large lemon tree in the front yard and an outhouse at the back of the garden. That was possibly one of the scariest places to visit at night. It's also the backyard where my pappou and yiayia would throw Sunday barbecues each week, with a spit going and cousins everywhere proudly standing on hosed-down concrete paving, and parsley shooting out from garden beds. My mum's name is Theodora Curran.

So, when I was born as their first child, I ended up with a name that brought both sides together. Traditionally, the first-born boy on the Greek side is named after the pappou and I was, because his name was Con. But to combine with my baba's heritage it became Conor. If we were going to switch everything and include my mum's maiden name, I would be called Kostantinos Mihali Makris, but I am happy with what I got, and love when people call me Con.

Baba's side never had a deep connection to their Irish heritage, and I was raised in my yiayia's Clifton Hill house as both my parents worked. This is where we would watch *Judge Judy* and *Jerry Springer* together as she cut apples for me, using a paring knife, before passing the slices over one by one. It's where we picked herbs in her garden and helped wash the parsley and tomatoes. It's where she would prepare kotopoulo me hilopites (chicken and pasta) and sit a slab of feta next to it for me to break off at my leisure. It's where all of this started and it's why this book exists. She passed a love for Greek food, traditions and culture to me, and I am incredibly grateful.

My yiayia Maria comes from the north of Peloponnese, in a spot called Aigio. It's a beachside area that when I visited was alive with locals holidaying and enjoying the beach. My pappou Con comes from a tiny village called Dafni, in the mountains of Peloponnese and only a two-hour drive from Aigio. The village of Dafni is a magical place, and luckily my pappou's family have gone back and rebuilt the house he grew up in. It sits on top of the village and overlooks the massive lake below. There is one tavern in the town and no shops, so every two days a fruit and vegetable truck will drive through the one-street town and beep along the way for you to come and grab all your produce. It's like stepping back in time whenever I return there. But funnily enough, my yiayia and pappou, despite growing up very close by to each other, didn't meet until after they moved to Melbourne.

Despite all of the above, I found myself resenting my Greek side. I was sent to a Greek Orthodox school for thirteen years, where Greek was intertwined into the curriculum. It wasn't a very fun place for someone who was Greek, but also very obviously queer. Being queer and Greek wasn't, and mostly still isn't, an easy journey. I was rejected and bullied, and it was a very dark time. Luckily, school isn't forever and after leaving high school, I was able to become myself, but being Greek had left a bad taste in my mouth. I visited the country and enjoyed island hopping, like many other Australians, but I didn't feel a connection like I thought I would, or more likely, didn't want to have.

The year 2020 came around and so did Covid. My career as a restaurant manager disappeared overnight, and all of sudden I was boxing up gourmet meals to be reheated at home for people across the state of Victoria. During this time, I applied for the show *MasterChef*, because I thought it would be really funny if I got to the judges' audition and got onto TV. Forever I would have an anecdote to pull out at the pub about that one time I got onto TV. Something crazy happened and I got through round after round before

I actually did make it to the judges' audition with my signature dish, Pan Asian spanakopita. It's a classic spiral spanakopita that gets broken off, piece by piece, and swiped through a Southeast Asian verde and fiery Vietnamese chilli sauce. Still to this day, I think the dish was pretty cool, but the judges did not. They said no to the dish and me getting an apron, but luckily there was a second-chance cook to get into the competition.

They asked me something that changed the trajectory of my life. 'Can you cook simple Greek food?' No, I thought to myself, I was always planning to do Southeast Asian food with some Greek influence, almost a fusion that has never been done, hence my social handle being 'Con-Fusion'. I had worked in Southeast Asian restaurants my whole life, and when I cooked – not often at all to be honest – it was generally using Asian ingredients. What I didn't realise at the time was how strong my knowledge of Greek food and cooking was; it was my entire upbringing. It was the food I ate day in and day out, and every celebration with family included Greek food. So, a day later I had a second chance to cook for the judges and after choosing the box with limited ingredients, I managed to cook a modern take on avgolemono (chicken egg lemon soup). It used King George whiting and a fish-bone broth instead of chicken, on top of thinly sliced nectarines and with a basil oil. I still don't know where that came from, but it landed me a spot in the top 24.

The rest is history. I went on to make winning dishes, like koulourakia olive oil ice-cream sandwiches, salmoriglio hilopites (pasta in verde sauce), olive oil cake with fig leaf ice-cream, braised octopus that celebrated six elements of lemon, and of course, kalamata olive ice-cream with cucumber granita that divided opinion among fans, but was loved by the judges. Being able to celebrate my heritage in a place that also celebrated me being queer was a watershed moment, which has led me here. Today, I can proudly say I can cook really good, simple and not-so-simple Greek food. And once you are cooking from this book, I hope you can say the exact same thing.

May you fall in love with Greek culture, Greek food and Greek cooking the way I fell back in love with it.

TO GO?

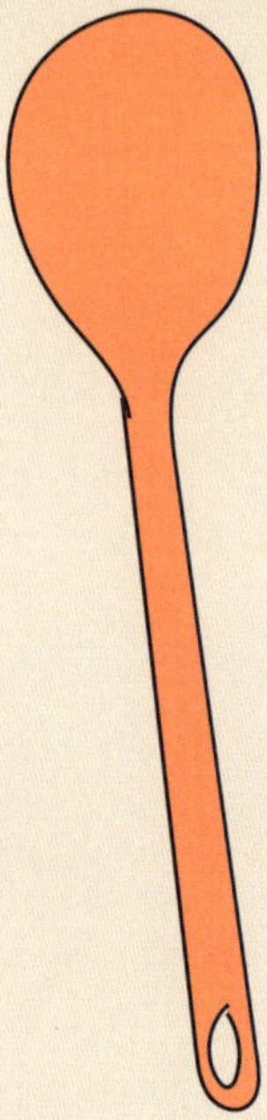

HOW I COOK

Naturally, everybody who cooks has a different method for how they go about recipes in their kitchen. This section is important to help you understand this cookbook, how to approach the recipes and the small intricacies in my wording to make sure when you cook these dishes they come out as delicious as possible.

HEAT

Temperature is one of the most important parts of cooking. Whether it be stove or oven, high or low and even the oven functions.

When I say 'heat a pan' or 'while the pan heats up', it means to allow the frying pan or saucepan to come up to the temperature mentioned. The five heats I will use for a stove are low, medium–low, medium, medium–high and high. If using an induction stovetop, this is easy to follow with the one to ten heat numbers. When using a gas stove, like I did when creating this book, use your judgement. I used only two hobs for all the recipes; one being the smallest hob and the other being the biggest hob. I played with the heats between these two.

All the recipes that use the oven will state the oven function. I always use fan-forced, unless otherwise stated. I also use the oven grill (broiler). This is such a great way to get some colour and char on food, so don't be afraid to use it. Everyone's oven is different, so keep an eye on the food when using the grill function.

MULTITASKING

When I cook, I generally tend to prep and cook as I go, because I feel comfortable in that space. If you follow the recipes, the method will let you know what to prep when and what to do next. Alternatively, if you enjoy being super organised, feel free to prep everything before you get started. There is no right or wrong way here, so do what feels natural.

DIETARIES

Looking for vegetarian or vegan recipes? Keep an eye out for the V (vegetarian) and VE (vegan) icons in the top right-hand corner of the recipe pages. Some recipes will also include a note on how to make a dish vegetarian or vegan by swapping or omitting ingredients.

(V) (VE)

INGREDIENTS

I want you to feel comfortable making natural swaps for preferences. If there's a fresh herb you don't love (like oregano or dill), fresh parsley is always a wonderful non-offensive swap-in. Can't access hilopites (Greek pasta) or can't be bothered making it fresh? Grab a similar dried pasta or a pasta shape you love and pair that with the pasta sauce in the recipe.

In savoury cooking, choosing your own adventure is fine, but I will warn you that when it comes to desserts or any baking, it's best to stick to the recipe. They are designed to work that way, and even a slight change can yield a very different result.

I am not here to shame you into buying high-quality, expensive ingredients. Purchase what you can and where you can. I like to spend my money on good fresh produce from markets. The garlic is better, the tomatoes are better, everything just tastes that bit more delicious. I would recommend buying a good extra-virgin olive oil to finish and dress dishes with, but always feel free to buy what you can and work with what you have at home.

FLAVOUR

You will notice some recipes go heavy on spices, herbs, lemon juice, salt and oil, and that's because I love getting hit with flavour when I eat food. If you are not a spice-driven person and find the woody spices a lot, try halving the measurements. This is where tasting as you go is very important. Always taste, and when it needs seasoning, do it to your taste. In recipes where there isn't a moment to taste before something gets cooked, I have included how much salt to add, but for recipes where you can check the seasoning as you go, using salt to taste reflects that.

NUTS

It's basically unheard of in Greek culture, but I have a nut allergy, which stems from my father's Irish side, with multiple uncles also allergic. This means the book is entirely nut free, and while that's not much of an issue when it comes to savoury Greek dishes, desserts are a different thing entirely. Walnuts, pistachios and almonds are all quite common, but I have managed to find delicious substitutes along my recipe-writing journey, such as my Nut-free baklava (page 174), which uses myriad seeds to create something incredibly similar to the original. Great if you're nut free like me, but also if nuts aren't an issue for you, I promise you won't miss them in my sweets!

And very importantly, if you get stuck on a term, technique or ingredient listed, or just want some more background on a dish, feel free to do some research. It takes seconds to find out information now, so take advantage of that. Also, make sure you know where you're heading before you begin cooking.

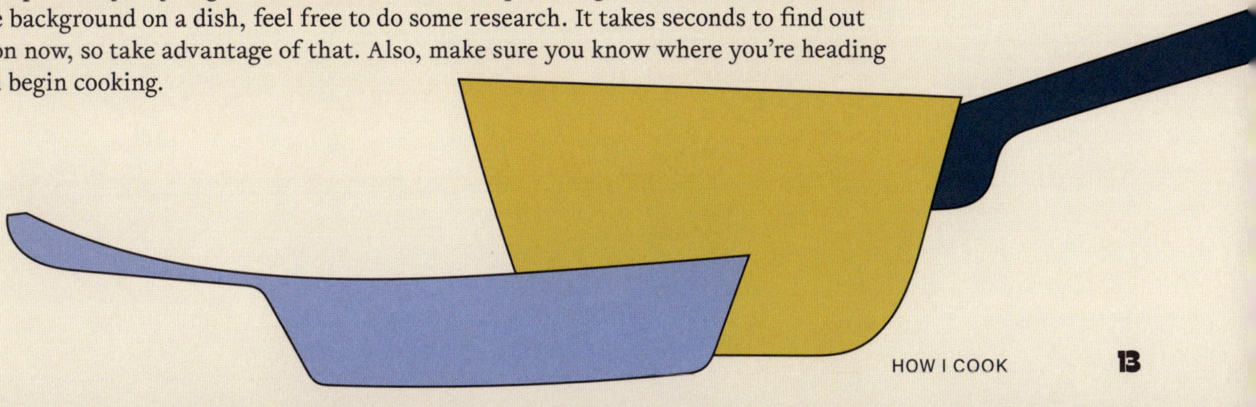

TO GO?
coffee,
sweets,
goods, and more
nephew

HOW I SHAKE

Cocktails and the world of mixology are just as interesting to me as the food side is. My years in hospitality allowed me to be behind bars, learning from some of the best. They took their time to walk me through the basics, the classics and why and how a few ingredients shaken or stirred with ice can turn into a complex and delicious sip.

Shaking cocktails at home is very different to shaking cocktails behind a bar. So, these tips are meant to help out in your kitchen, and hopefully take the fear out of whipping up cocktails at home. There is nothing more chic than a curated cocktail to start off a dinner party. As you venture into my cocktail recipes, find what suits your tastebuds the best and give it a go.

When it comes to my tastebuds, you'll notice a lot of savoury ingredients make their way into my drinks. Don't fear, my cocktail objective is that they remain balanced and maybe venture a tiny bit towards savoury, or sometimes punchy or sweeter, but they all should be balanced. Savoury ingredients create a wonderful intrigue, and make your brain take a second to register. It's one of the reasons why I love infusing savoury flavours into desserts as well.

FUNDAMENTALS

Generally, with cocktails you can either shake, stir or build.

There is a wet shake, which is a hard shake in a cocktail shaker with ice for 12–15 seconds, and a dry shake, which is in a shaker without ice for 12–15 seconds. The dry shake is very common in sours, where the purpose is to foam the egg white/aquafaba, as well as allowing the citrus juice and egg white to hit each other with force. The heat created by the movement helps to 'cook' the egg white. It's not dissimilar to using citrus to 'cook' fish for ceviche.

A stirred cocktail is when the liquid ingredients are stirred down with ice over time. These generally tend to be boozier numbers, like the martini or old fashioned, and feature spirits, liqueurs and syrups. The ice dilutes them gently until perfectly palatable.

Finally, the build is considered the easiest-of-all cocktail, where ingredients are thrown into a glass one by one and built on top of each other, maybe with a stir as you go. The most popular stirred cocktail is the mojito. It's a great shout when you have a lot of drinks to make and not a lot of shakers to go around.

EQUIPMENT

I always suggest investing in a Boston cocktail shaker. It differs from the more popular cobbler, which has a strainer already attached. The Boston results in a much cleaner product. With a Boston shaker, you'll also need to have a Hawthorne strainer and fine-mesh strainer to get a speak-easy level result. In my recipes, you will also see me say 'double strain'. That means pouring the cocktail through both the Hawthorne and fine-mesh strainers at the same time. Now, I know a lot of you beginner cocktail makers will naturally head to the cobbler shaker, but I implore you to test yourself with the two-piece Boston. Once you get the hang of it, you'll never look back.

When it comes to the extras, a long bar spoon, a multi-millilitre jigger and a solid juicer are also good investments. Make sure your freezer can hold a lot of ice – cocktails go through ice like no one's business. Don't be afraid to make what I call the 'share house swaps'. This is swapping high-end equipment for whatever you have lying around and making do. No shaker? Add everything to a jar and shake hard. No fine-mesh strainer? Whip out your everyday large mesh strainer. No bar spoon? A chopstick works so well, and sometimes it's my preferred choice. No sugar syrups? Grab that jar of jam forgotten at the back of your fridge.

BALANCING

To me, making cocktails is like balancing flavours. You have your base spirit, flavoured liqueurs, citrus juice and syrups. Sometimes fresh fruit gets muddled in, and now and again fresh herbs get shaken through. The best and most effective way to get different, unusual flavours into cocktails is by simmering them in sugar syrups. That's why you'll see them throughout my book. Most cocktails have a syrup added in. It's usually a very small amount, so don't be afraid of the sugar.

Everyone's tastebuds are different, and what you enjoy will be different to the next person. To get cocktails closer to what you want: if it's too sweet, add citrus; if it's too sour, add sugar syrup; if it's too strong, water it down a little bit; and if it's got too sweet and sour, add in a touch more alcohol. Always remember to taste and trust your palate.

SIMPLE SUGAR SYRUP

A simple sugar syrup is made with sugar and water. People will generally have a 1:1 ratio, but coming from a bar background, I have always known it to be 2:1 sugar to water, allowing a strong sweetness without diluting the cocktail too much.

To create the syrup, place 1 cup (220 g) caster (superfine) sugar in a heatproof bowl. Boil the kettle, then pour ½ cup (125 ml) boiling water over the sugar. Using a spoon, quickly mix it all together until the sugar has dissolved. Pour the syrup into a sterilised, heatproof airtight container and store in the fridge for up to a year (for how to sterilise, see Notes page 39). This amount will make eighteen to twenty cocktails.

NEXT LEVEL

Here are some quick tips to take your home cocktails to a whole new level. While these might seem like small things, collectively they make all the difference.

CHILL THE GLASSWARE

Even if it's into the freezer for just a few moments of chilling, cold cocktails should always be served in chilled glasses, just as hot food goes onto hot plates in restaurants.

PREP THE GARNISHES

Have your garnishes ready to go. Check out online videos on how to create special toppers from citrus peel. You drink with your eyes, and a wonderful garnish can truly be the cherry on top of your masterpiece.

USE FRESH INGREDIENTS

When it comes to herbs, eggs and fruits, fresh is so important. Slightly wilted herbs will ruin a cocktail, so steer clear. A fresh egg white is really important to get the foamiest drink possible.

RESEARCH SPIRITS

Not all spirits are made equal. Some are better than others. Don't spend a fortune on them, but find a solid quality all-rounder that won't overpower the cocktail. Australia produces some wonderful gins, for example, but a lot are flavoured with strong botanicals, whereas a classic dry London gin works wonderfully in cocktails because it doesn't take over.

INVEST IN GLASSWARE

High-quality glasses, particularly coupes, are very special. Head to a hospitality shop to source them for a great price. Venues need excellent glassware and have to deal with regular breakages, so a hospitality supplier is a great place to grab the exact same glasses.

MAKE IT REUSABLE

Whether it be straws or cocktail picks, buy steel or brass ones, as you'll have them forever. Also, they just look stunning against cocktail creations and make it that little bit more luxe.

INGREDIENTS

FETA CHEESE

Feta can differ in quality, but the main and easiest way to find better feta is to make sure it is spelled with one 't' rather than two. Cheese spelt 'feta' must be made in Greece, and as such will be a little more expensive. The dishes where you can get away with the cheaper 'fetta' are where the cheese is cooked, as opposed to being used fresh.

FIGS AND FIG LEAVES

Fig trees are a magical plant that I love watching through the seasons – from bare in winter, to the bountiful leaves and fruit by autumn. Fig leaves are an ingredient I became familiar with on *MasterChef*. The leaves are a wonderful and free way to flavour syrups and milk-based desserts (if you have a lovely neighbour that will let you grab some). The leaves are nutty and figgy, with a luscious coconut undertone. I recommend playing around with them when fig trees are producing the leaves.

FILO PASTRY

I love filo pastry, and I used to love making it from scratch, but it is really time consuming, so I purchase Antoniou – it's my preferred brand. It comes at fridge temperature, so you don't need to thaw it. It's just really excellent quality. If not available, use what you can find, but make sure to completely thaw any frozen pastry before using it or it will break.

GARLIC

Every recipe in this book uses garlic bought from a grocer or market, and as such the cloves are a lot bigger than the ones you find at the supermarket. If using supermarket garlic, you may need two cloves to every one stated in the recipe. If using jarred minced garlic, as a general rule 1 teaspoon minced garlic is equal to 1 garlic clove.

HERBS

Vibrant green herbs are the backbone of Greek cooking. You'll notice fresh oregano, mint, parsley and a lot of dill throughout the book. Not everyone is going to vibe with each herb, so feel free to swap herbs for something similar that you enjoy. Parsley is always an easy, non-offensive swap if in doubt.

When using fresh herbs, make sure to wash them properly and dry, and don't forget to check if the recipe includes the stems or not. With parsley and dill, where the leaves are at the top, a lot of the time I include the stems due to pure laziness. With leaves like mint and oregano, the taste of the stems isn't great, so take care not to leave a bit of stem when you should only use the leaves.

I buy my herbs from grocers, which I prefer for abundance – you'll have more to play with. Supermarket herbs are fine in terms of flavour, but you may need two bunches to fulfil the recipe.

For oregano, I prefer to use dried mountain oregano, but regular dried leaves are fine as well.

KALAMATA OLIVES

I recommend purchasing an olive pitter and buying unpitted olives as the flavour is so delicious. They're also usually cheaper. If time poor, hit up a high-quality pitted kalamata.

KEFALOGRAVIERA CHEESE

Very popular in Greece, this hard yellow cheese is wonderfully nutty and is becoming more readily available in supermarkets. It's a blend between kefalotyri and graviera cheeses. I generally use it in place of parmesan. If you struggle to source it, check out the recipe notes for suitable substitutes.

LEMON

My love of lemon will shock no one. It is incredibly versatile; it can be used in savoury and sweet, and there are so many ways to use it, from the juice to the zest. Always remember the delicious flavour will get cooked out over time, so finishing dishes with lemon juice is advised (unless it's being slowly cooked in the juice). The zest is a wonderful way to impart lemony goodness during the cook, as the oil and zest meld into the food.

If the recipe asks for the zest, don't chuck out the zested lemon as there's a good chance you will need it later on for the juice. Got extra citrus? Use it up in a salad dressing, like my Greek goddess (page 48) or Classic (page 50).

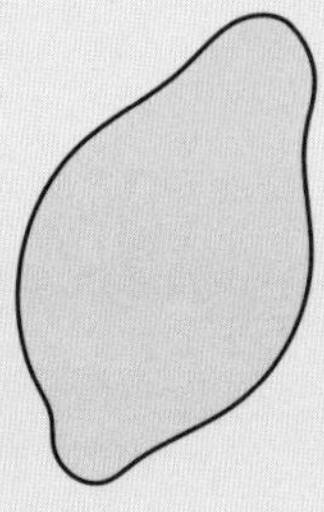

MASTIHA

Resin harvested from the mastic tree is what creates the beautiful liqueur known as mastiha. It's a sweeter Greek liqueur, with lovely pine and woody notes that go so well in cocktails. If you're not on the anise train, I recommend grabbing a mastiha and giving it a go. It creates cocktails like you've never had before, as the mastic is such an untouched flavour in the world of bartending.

OILS

There are three oils that you will need to cook my recipes.

The first one is olive oil. When you see olive oil listed in the ingredients list, it is used just for cooking purposes. I recommend just grabbing a cheap extra-virgin olive oil for this.

The second oil is high-quality extra-virgin olive oil, also known as the dressing and finishing oil. This will be the most expensive oil, but I only use it in small amounts, so you can enjoy all the benefits and the lovely flavour.

The third is a neutral oil – my choice is canola oil – for frying and emulsifying. Cheap to purchase and great for frying food, it is also used to help emulsify sauces as it has a neutral and non-offensive taste to it.

OUZO

This very divisive spirit is one of my favourites, and I implore you to give it a shot in my recipes. A good ouzo will have a warming anise flavour, and is beautiful over ice and sipped slowly. If you can't get on board with it, I won't hold it against you. Look to swap it for a more citrus herbal spirit, like Lillet Blanc or a different aperitif spirit that you enjoy, like Campari or Pimm's.

SALT

There are two salts I use in this cookbook.

The first one is a cheap cooking salt. All my recipes have been cooked using this salt, so unless specified otherwise, this is the salt to throw in. Cooking salt is very salty, so make sure to add it in pinches bit by bit to your taste, and layer the flavour of salt through the dish over time.

The other one is flaky sea salt, a wonderful, but pricier, option. This is a great way to finish a dish, and is wonderful with chocolate or caramel in desserts. It has a milder flavour, but because it is more expensive, I reserve it for the finishing of dishes. The light saltiness helps bring out the final flavour of the dish.

SPICES

Greece is very fortunate because of its location as a historical crossroads of trade routes. This meant spices very quickly integrated into Greek food and recipes. Dried oregano is the most common, but brown spices, such as allspice, cumin, cinnamon, nutmeg and clove, are just as important. Red sauces are so different throughout Greece. Where you were from would determine what spices you had access to. My family has always used allspice in plentiful amounts in savoury cooking, and it's one of my favourites to combine with dried oregano – they go so well together. My recipes also feature cinnamon, nutmeg and clove in not just sweet cooking, but more predominantly in savoury dishes and slow braises. These add a sweet, warming depth – a special layer of complexity that I really appreciate in Greek cooking.

MAKE THE MENU

If you've ever visited Greece you will understand the importance of sharing food with the ones you love. It's a ritual, a way of life and there is always time made for sharing a meal. Families, cousins, friends, partners and everyone in between flock to tavernas and each other's houses well into the night for a dinner, a few wines and maybe tsipouro, a Greek brandy. Every time I have visited my cousins in Greece, everything is put on hold so we can all sit and have a late lunch together filled with plates of classic Greek dishes. It's special and something a lot of the world has lost, but there is always time to bring it back. So, these menus are designed for whatever meal experience you want to have with your family or chosen family. Drop a recipe if it's too much, improvise the menu, create your own, go low effort or high, but the most important rule is that you enjoy yourself as well.

A BIG FAT GREEK EASTER

SERVES 6–8

Orthodox Easter is my favourite celebration on the Greek calendar, so why shouldn't non-Greeks get to enjoy the best part about it too? The food. Everything centres around the slow-cooked lamb shoulder that falls off the bone. Paired with the classic Greek salad and tzatziki, it's the perfect combination of flavours on a plate. Batch up the cocktail and just pour it over ice. It means less work for you and more time to kick back.

Cocktail (to start): Hard lemonade (page 130) or Mastiha spritz (page 84)
Small shared plate: Tzatziki (page 210)
Small shared plate: Maria's burnt peas (page 121)
Large shared plate: Oregano lamb shoulder (page 193)
Side: Classic Greek salad (page 46)
Light dessert: Easter biscuits (page 123)

WINE BAR VIBES

SERVES 6–10

Who doesn't love to just snack their way through a menu? As all the Melbourne kids will know, the European wine bar has become a staple in our fair city, and as such it's only apt that you turn your own space into the hottest new spot where it's very invite only. The one rule with these recipes is that they have to be easy to grab and eaten in a few quick bites. Head to your local wine merchant for a selection of assyrtiko and agiorgitiko wines, make a cheeseboard of kefalotyri and manouri cheeses, pre-batch the negronis and set out the bites.

Cocktail: Kanelada negroni (page 77)
Snack: Roasted olives (page 90)
Snack: Feta and olive focaccia (page 138)
Snack: Beetroot tzatziki (page 213)
Snack: Grilled bullhorn peppers (page 102)
Light dessert: Compressed ouzo watermelon (page 218)

BOUGIE SET DINNER

SERVES 4

The overachiever of the group? If you are a Capricorn like me, look no further than the Bougie Set Dinner. This is for the old-school, nineties style of dining: an entree, main and dessert, a cocktail to start and finish. And the best part is a lot of the work is pre-done, so you get to enjoy yourself and still receive the applause once those dessert spoons hit the empty plates.

Cocktail (to start): Feta and kalamata martini (page 228)
Entree: Beef tartare (page 33)
Main: Tomato baked fish (page 149)
Side: Lettuce salad (page 52)
Dessert: Yoghurt panna cotta and spiced strawberries (page 220)
Cocktail (to finish): Fig leaf old fashioned (page 224)

I CAN'T AFFORD A EUROPEAN HOLIDAY

SERVES 4–6

Just because you can't get to Europe, doesn't mean you can't bring Europe to you. A lot of my food is inspired by the countries that surround Greece, so these dishes are connected in origin to Italy, France, Turkey and Spain, meaning you and your guests can get the whole Mediterranean energy in one menu.

Cocktail (to start): Greek mulled wine (page 132)
Snack: Greek skewers (page 30)
Main: Chicken Marbella la Greca (page 214)
Side: Turkish grain salad (page 106)
Side: Glazed carrots (page 94)
Dessert: Lemon tiramisu (page 199)

THE ISLAND HOPPER

SERVES 4–6

Seafood and the smell of the ocean hitting you from every direction is where I want this menu to transport you. It's a collection of recipes the Greek Islands are known for, whether it's dakos (rusk tomato salad) from Crete, braised octopus or portokalopita (whole orange filo cake) from Milos. These dishes feature in every island taverna, with seafood caught fresh that morning and braised or grilled to perfection. The menu is designed to share (like all of my food), so make it all and let your mates tuck in.

Cocktail (to start): Santorini sour (page 74)
Small shared plate: Fava dip (page 98) and Pita bread (page 169)
Medium shared plate: Simple fish (page 58)
Large shared plate: Braised octopus (page 117), served with Zhoug green sauce (page 100)
Side: Cretan rusk tomato salad (page 57)
Dessert: Whole orange filo cake (page 200)

Clockwise from top left: Pita bread, Cretan rusk tomato salad, Simple fish, Santorini sour, Braised octopus with Zhoug green sauce, Whole orange filo cake and Fava dip.

20–30 MINUTES

I HAVE LIMITED TIME

TIME IS NOT ALWAYS YOUR FRIEND,

especially with life being so busy – generally busier than we'd like. These recipes clock in at under 30 minutes, so they're perfect for lunches and quick weekend snacks. There are also a few speedy numbers for when mates are coming over and you've left everything to the last second.

Time
25 minutes

GREEK SKEWERS

MAKES 20

GILDAS

20 pitted Sicilian green olives
10 pickled peppers (see Notes)
3 large pieces roasted red capsicum (pepper, see Notes)
20 anchovies
20 cocktail skewers

WHIPPED ORANGE FETA
1 orange
200 g (7 oz) feta cheese
1 teaspoon dried oregano

Notes

- To make these skewers vegetarian, omit the anchovies.
- I've used pickled Greek golden peppers here, but any type of pickled pepper will work.
- If using store-bought roasted capsicum, choose a high-quality brand. Alternatively, make the Pickled peppers (page 226).

This punchy skewer is what I want when I wander into a mate's dinner party. Traditionally, a gilda is a Spanish dish comprised of a pickled guindilla pepper, anchovy and olive – the combination just works. For my version, I wanted to celebrate the original but give it a new vibe. The addition of roasted capsicum (pepper) gives it a smoky hit and a bit of sweetness that holds it together. The whipped orange feta is way better than it should be; try the leftovers on toast and thank me later.

To make the whipped orange feta, finely grate the zest of the orange into a food processor. Add the feta and oregano, and process until combined. Cut the orange into quarters, then squeeze in the juice of 1 quarter. Process until smooth and thick. Spoon the whipped orange feta into a piping bag.

Pipe the whipped feta into the olives.

Halve the peppers and slice the capsicum into thick strips.

Now, don't feel like you have to follow the order I have used, but thread the olives, anchovies and capsicum and pepper pieces onto 20 cocktail skewers. Serve.

BEEF TARTARE

Time
25 minutes

SERVES 2–4 (AS A SHARED STARTER)

- 30 g (1 oz) dill pickle
- 1 small French shallot
- 10 g (⅓ oz) fresh chives
- 5 g (⅛ oz) fresh oregano leaves
- 30 g (1 oz) baby capers, chopped
- 200 g (7 oz) beef rump steak (see Note)
- 1 tablespoon extra-virgin olive oil
- 2 teaspoons Dijon mustard
- 80 g (2¾ oz) salted potato chips (crisps)

Note
I really love rump steak for this recipe. It has great flavour and is tender. I strongly recommend visiting your local butcher for some quality beef – it needs to be as fresh as possible.

This is a dish that seems scarier to make than it actually is. Living in Melbourne, I have watched every restaurant give it a spin with their own take. This is my slightly Greek beef tartare. I didn't want to venture too far from the classic, but the little additions of fresh oregano and dill pickle give it a whole new identity. It's a great starter for entertaining or to share with someone before dinner. The only way to make this even better would be if you flew to Greece and bought a packet of oregano potato chips to serve with it, but simple salted chips work well too.

Finely chop the pickle, shallot, chives and oregano, and add them all to a bowl. Stir in the capers until combined.

Clean up the beef by removing any fat or sinew. Using a sharp knife, gently cut the beef into thin slices, then collect the strips together and finely dice. Add to the pickle mixture, along with the oil and mustard. Season with salt if it needs it and stir until combined.

To serve, spoon the beef mixture onto a large serving plate. Arrange the chips on one side, then use the chips to scoop up the beef tartare.

Time
15 minutes

FRIED KEFALOGRAVIERA CHEESE (V)

SERVES 2 (AS A SHARED STARTER)

SAGANAKI

30 g (1 oz) honey
30 ml (1 fl oz) fresh lemon juice, plus extra lemon wedge to serve
30 ml (1 fl oz) ouzo (see Notes)
100 g (3½ oz) piece kefalograviera cheese (see Notes)
2 tablespoons plain (all-purpose) flour
Olive oil
1 tablespoon dried oregano

Notes

- If you can't find ouzo, Pernod or sambuca, which are also anise-flavoured liqueurs, will also work.
- You can absolutely also make this alcohol free – just use the same amount of water instead of ouzo.
- Make sure the kefalograviera is cold and straight from the fridge. If it's too warm, it won't hold its structure while cooking.
- When flipping the cheese, the thinner the spatula the better as you don't want to smoosh the crust that forms while cooking.
- This is a great dish to serve with fresh fruit, like figs. You could also add finely diced peach and fresh thyme leaves to the syrup.

I am going to clarify something here: saganaki refers to the small, heavy-based frying pan used to fry dishes. This is why you'll see dishes like prawn saganaki – where cheese has nothing to do with the word saganaki. Over time in restaurants, the word 'saganaki' has come to mean a gooey, charred piece of Greek cheese that you hit with lemon to punch through the sweetness of the honey and the fattiness of the cheese. It's gobbled up as a starter before getting into a Greek feast. Here is my recipe for the best saganaki. My honey mixture uses equal parts honey, lemon juice and ouzo.

Place the honey, lemon juice and ouzo in a jar. Seal and shake super hard to bring it together.

Place a small, heavy-based, non-stick frying pan over high heat. Coat the kefalograviera in the flour. Shake off the excess. Heat some oil in the pan. Add the cheese and cook for 90 seconds–2 minutes, or until caramelised around the edges.

Using a thin spatula (see Notes), flip the cheese and cook for a further 1–2 minutes. Pour the honey mixture around the cheese and cook for a further minute. Gently spoon the syrup over the cheese. Take off the heat.

To serve, either plate up with the syrup on top or serve it in the pan (which is more traditional). Sprinkle with the oregano, serve with the extra lemon wedge and fight over it with someone you love.

HALLOUMI, TOMATO AND PEACH (V)

Time
30 minutes

SERVES 4 (AS A SHARED STARTER)

250–300 g (9–10½ oz) piece halloumi
1 tablespoon extra-virgin olive oil, plus extra for drizzling
1 small French shallot
1 yellow peach
2 tomatoes
3 fresh basil sprigs
½ lemon
1 garlic clove
Salt and cracked black pepper, to taste
Fresh bread, to serve

Many restaurant menus have dripping wet burrata as a starter, but I think it's time halloumi took its place. The fact that halloumi can take a hard char without falling apart makes it suited to cooking like a protein. Pretend the halloumi is a steak for this recipe. Grill it hard over high heat on all six sides, then gently cook it through in the oven. It will leave a smoky, melt-in-your-mouth finish while keeping its wonderful structure. Pair it with bright tomatoes and peaches to create a delicious starter for you and your mates.

Preheat oven to 200°C (400°F) fan-forced.

Pat dry the halloumi with paper towel. Heat a heavy-based, non-stick frying pan over medium–high heat. Add the oil to the middle of the pan and once hot, add the halloumi, pushing down with tongs, for 45 seconds, or until very charred. (You want an almost burnt, very dark brown colour.) Turn and cook the halloumi on all six sides until charred and caramelised. Take off the heat.

Transfer the halloumi to a baking tray and bake for 15–20 minutes, or until it can be easily pierced with a knife. (The longer the better to get softer halloumi – you don't want it squeaky.)

Meanwhile, prep the salad. Finely dice the shallot, cut the peach and tomatoes into medium cubes and pick and roughly tear the basil leaves. Place them all in a bowl. Squeeze in the juice of the lemon half. Mince the garlic, then place it in a separate small bowl, along with a drizzle of extra oil. Season with salt and pepper. Pour the garlic mixture over the salad. Mix through, then place in the fridge until ready to serve.

Place the halloumi in the middle of a shallow serving bowl or deep plate. Spoon the salad around the halloumi. Pour over any dressing left in the bowl. Serve with fresh bread and enjoy all together, with a small knife to cut open the halloumi.

GREEK SCRAMBLED EGGS (V)

Time
20 minutes

SERVES 1

STRAPATSADA

2 large tomatoes
2 garlic cloves
1 tablespoon olive oil, plus extra for drizzling
1 teaspoon dried oregano
2 eggs
Salt, to taste
25 g (1 oz) feta cheese
Crusty bread, to serve

This Greek take on shakshuka is ten times easier and faster than the original. Strapatsada is a tomato scrambled eggs, and it's a traditional breakfast in Greece. For a recipe with such a short ingredient list, you'd be surprised by how many different ways this can be cooked. Some like to slowly cook the eggs and tomato together, while others prefer to use charred cherry tomatoes. Mine brings a modern sensibility to the dish without taking away the nostalgia. I've removed as much liquid as possible to give it more flavour. And don't skip the feta! It really brings the dish together.

Grate the tomatoes into a bowl, discarding the skin.

Thinly slice the garlic.

Heat a frying pan over medium–low heat, then add the oil and let it heat up for 30 seconds. Add the garlic and oregano, and gently sizzle, stirring with a silicone spatula, for 1 minute. Add the grated tomato and stir until combined. Increase heat to medium and cook for 10 minutes. Season with salt.

While the tomato sauce comes together, crack the eggs into a bowl and whisk together.

Once most of the liquid from the tomato has evaporated, push the mixture to one side of the pan. Increase heat to high and add a drizzle more oil. Give it a minute to heat up, then pour in the egg. Gently mix together with the tomato sauce so you create egg ribbons. When the egg is no longer runny, take off the heat.

Finish by crumbling feta on top and serve with crusty bread.

CHILLI OLIVE TAPENADE (VE)

Time
10 minutes

MAKES 1 JAR

2 long fresh red chillies
250 g (9 oz) pitted kalamata olives
4 garlic cloves
1 tablespoon baby capers
20 g (¾ oz) fresh flat-leaf (Italian) parsley leaves
2 tablespoons neutral oil (see Notes)
1 tablespoon white vinegar
Salt, to taste

Notes

- Sunflower oil is best for this recipe.
- The tapenade will last for up to a week in the fridge.
- How to sterilise a jar or container: Before filling the jar, I make sure it goes through a hot dishwasher twice to sterilise it. There are many methods for doing this, like adding to boiling water for 20 minutes, but I find the dishwasher easiest.

TASTES EVEN BETTER THE NEXT DAY

A good, solid olive tapenade is incredibly underrated. It's really easy to put together and goes great on a cheese board, as a punchy spread in sandwiches or as a flavour-bomb topping for protein. Chilli adds a hint of heat that takes it to another level. I am big fan of eating it with halloumi – like on my THAT sandwich (page 42) as it punches through the fattiness of the cheese. Now, I use whole chillies with seeds, but if you prefer it less spicy, feel free to remove the seeds. This tapenade is only mildly hot to begin with, as long red chillies aren't too spicy.

Remove the stems from the chillies, then place the chillies in a food processor, along with the remaining ingredients and a pinch of salt. Process on high until everything is blitzed together and the mixture is deep purple.

Transfer tapenade to a sterilised jar (see Notes). Serve as a spread or dip.

GREEK FRY-UP

Time
30 minutes

SERVES 2

400 g (14 oz) frozen potato gems
2 loukaniko sausages (see Notes)
1 large tomato
Olive oil
1 brown onion
3 garlic cloves
1 teaspoon dried oregano, plus extra to serve
1 teaspoon ground cinnamon
1 teaspoon ground paprika
400 g (14 oz) tin butter (lima) beans, rinsed and drained (see Notes)
400 g (14 oz) tin diced tomatoes
2 eggs
Salt, to taste
80 g (2¾ oz) feta cheese

Notes

- If you can't find loukaniko, good-quality pork sausages with fennel seeds or orange zest will work.
- Traditionally, this dish is made with large butter (lima) beans, but you can use any cooked, tinned white beans, such as cannellini.
- There will be some gigantes left over. Place them in the fridge and enjoy the next day.

The ol' big breakfast fry-up. It has nursed me through many Sunday mornings, particularly during the years I lived in London – but it's even better with a Greek twist. It was a staple in my yiayia's house to fry potatoes cut into chips, pop a large fried egg on top, then sprinkle with oregano and crumbled feta. We'd dunk chips into the egg yolk like soldiers. This is similar, but with potato gems (the GOAT/greatest of all time in the frozen potato world), loukaniko (Greek sausages made with fennel seeds and orange zest) and, of course, gigantes (the Greek answer to baked beans). Gigantes are soaked lima beans baked in a lightly spiced red sauce. This is my quick version; it has the same vibe, but is perfect for a speedy breakfast fry-up.

Preheat oven to 180°C (350°F) fan-forced. Line a baking tray with baking paper.

Place the potato gems and sausages on the prepared tray. Halve the tomato and add, cut-side up, to the tray. Drizzle with oil. Sprinkle a pinch of salt over the tomato halves. Roast for 20 minutes, turning the potato gems and sausages halfway through.

Meanwhile, begin working on the gigantes. Heat a large saucepan over medium–high heat. Add a drizzle of oil. Thinly slice the onion, then add to the pan with a pinch of salt. Sauté for 3 minutes. Increase heat to high. Mince the garlic and add to the pan, along with the oregano, cinnamon, paprika and beans. Cook, stirring, for 1 minute. Add the tinned tomatoes and stir until combined. Bring to the boil, then reduce heat to low and cook for 15 minutes. After 15 minutes, the gigantes mixture should be reduced and thickened.

Using the back of a spoon, make two cavities in the gigantes mixture, then crack an egg into each cavity. Cover and cook for 5 minutes, or until the egg is just cooked through.

While the egg is cooking, switch the oven to grill (broiler) on 250°C (500°F). Grill everything on the tray for 5 minutes to get some caramelisation.

To serve, place the sausages, tomato, potato gems and eggs with the gigantes on a serving plate. Top with the feta and sprinkle with extra oregano. Dunk the potato gems in the egg yolk and feta, with the roasted tomato as a saucy accompaniment to the sausage.

THAT (V)

Time
20 minutes

(TAPENADE, HALLOUMI, AVOCADO, TOMATO)

SERVES 2

1 large tomato
1 avocado
½ lemon
2 tablespoons olive oil
150 g (5½ oz) piece halloumi
Salt, to taste
2 milk buns (see Note)
½ cup (30 g) Chilli olive tapenade (see page 39)

Note
Feel free to toast the halved buns under the oven grill (broiler) or using a chargrill pan, depending on your preference.

The BLAT is a well-loved brunch staple that has been elevated over the years. Traditionally, it's done with bacon, lettuce, avocado and tomato, and makes a pretty bomb sandwich. But this is what happens when a Greek gets hold of an idea; I present you my version of the BLAT, and I call it a THAT! It features tapenade, halloumi, avocado and tomato, creating the greatest evolution in sandwich history. It's become a must-have for my partner and I on Saturday mornings. I really recommend grabbing some fresh buns to put it with. Start the weekend out right.

Thinly slice the tomato.

Mash the avocado in a bowl. Squeeze in the juice of the lemon half. Add 1 tablespoon oil and stir until combined. Season with salt.

Heat a heavy-based frying pan over medium–high heat, then add the remaining 1 tablespoon oil. Slice the halloumi in half lengthways, then add to the pan. Reduce heat to medium and cook, not moving the halloumi pieces, for 2 minutes, or until golden and beginning to melt in the middle. Flip and cook for a further 2 minutes, or until golden.

To build the sandwich, halve the buns and spoon the avocado mixture onto the bun bases. Top with the halloumi, tomato slices and tapenade. Sandwich with the bun tops.

GRILLED CHEESE AND OLIVES (V)

Time
20 minutes

MAKES 1

8 pitted kalamata olives
1 long pickled pepper (see Notes)
30 g (1 oz) kefalograviera cheese (see Notes)
40 g (1½ oz) gruyere cheese
2 bread slices
2 tablespoons mayonnaise

Notes

- Pickled peppers are very common in Greek dishes. They can be found in most supermarkets in hot and mild varieties.
- If you can't find kefalograviera cheese, grab kefalotyri or look for saganaki at the shops, as saganaki usually refers to either of these cheeses.
- Spreading mayonnaise, instead of oil or butter, on the top and bottom of the bread is the best way to get a high-quality golden crust and lovely sear on your grilled sandwich.

Kalamata olives and yellow cheese has been a favourite combination of mine ever since I can remember. When I was younger, I would get home from school and top a bunch of rice crackers with olives and grated cheese, pop them in the microwave and enjoy as a snack. There are a million ways to make grilled cheese, and everyone proclaims their way is the best, but I reckon mine is solid. It's unlike anything you've ever had because of the two cheeses you don't generally see together. The gruyere is rich, creamy and has a higher melting point, whereas the kefalograviera is harder and nuttier, with a tangy hit that's really welcomed in a grilled cheese.

Slice the olives and pepper into 5 mm (¼ in) pieces.

Coarsely grate the cheeses into a bowl and stir until combined.

Spread one side of each slice of bread with the mayonnaise (see Notes). Sandwich together the mayonnaise-side of the slices to stop them sticking to the bench while you assemble. Build the filling by placing a layer of grated cheese on the top bread slice, then all the olive and pepper pieces. Finish with the remaining cheese.

Place a non-stick frying pan with a lid over medium heat. Carefully peel off the bottom bread slice and place the top slice with all the fillings in the pan, mayonnaise-side down. Top with the remaining slice, mayonnaise-side up. Sizzle, pushing down with a spatula to keep everything tight, for 2–3 minutes, or until there's a nice golden char on the bottom. Carefully flip the sandwich and cook for a further 1 minute–90 seconds, or until golden. Add a splash of water to the pan and cover with the lid. Cook for a further 1–2 minutes, or until the cheese is melted.

Cut in half to serve.

TUNA MELT LA GRECA

Time
30 minutes

MAKES 2

1 large French shallot
15 g (½ oz) fresh flat-leaf (Italian) parsley sprigs
15 g (½ oz) fresh dill
20 pitted kalamata olives
½ lemon
425 g (15 oz) tin tuna in springwater, drained
⅓ cup (85 g) mayonnaise, plus extra for spreading
50 g (1¾ oz) kefalograviera cheese (see Notes)
60 g (2¼ oz) mozzarella cheese
4 dill pickles
4 sourdough or rye bread slices
Salt and cracked black pepper, to taste
2 long pickled peppers (store-bought or for homemade, see page 226), for garnishing

Notes

- Kefalograviera is a hard Greek cheese with a nutty taste. It's what gives this sandwich such a great bite. It is used for the Greek dish saganaki, which is what the packet might say in some supermarkets. If you can't find any, pecorino will mimic it well, or you can just use extra mozzarella for a meltier result.
- Spreading mayonnaise, instead of oil or butter, on the top and bottom of the bread is the best way to get a high-quality golden crust and lovely sear on your grilled sandwich.
- You may have some tuna mixture left over. Store in an airtight container in the fridge for up to 4 days.

If there is anything I know from living in inner-city Melbourne, it's that we all love a sandwich. Melbourne took it to another level in recent years, but there will always be something so lovely about making it yourself (it's a bit cheaper as well). This is my Greek take on the tuna melt, my favourite go-to sandwich. The tuna mix is plumped up with olives and herbs, and the parsley stems give it a wonderful texture. The mix of kefalograviera and mozzarella gives the sandwich a nutty bite, as well as that lovely, melty cheese stretch.

Finely chop the shallot, parsley leaves and stems (the stems add great texture and crunch to the mix), and dill, and transfer them all to a bowl. Roughly chop the olives and add to the bowl. Squeeze in the juice of the lemon half. Add the tuna and mayonnaise, season with salt and pepper, then mix together.

Coarsely grate the cheeses into a bowl and stir until combined.

Thinly slice the dill pickles.

Spread extra mayonnaise over 2 bread slices (see Notes). Sandwich together the mayonnaise-side of the slices together to stop them sticking to the bench while you assemble. Build the filling by placing half the cheese on the top bread slice. Top with half the pickle slices and one-third of the tuna mixture (or an amount that makes sense for your sandwich). Repeat with more extra mayonnaise and the remaining bread slices, cheese, pickle and tuna mixture to build a second tuna melt.

Place a non-stick frying pan with a lid over medium heat. Working with one sandwich, carefully peel off the bottom bread slice and place the top slice with the fillings in the pan, mayonnaise-side down. Top with the remaining slice, mayonnaise-side up. Sizzle, pushing down with a spatula to keep everything tight, for 2–3 minutes, or until there's a nice golden char on the bottom. Carefully flip the sandwich and cook for a further 1 minute–90 seconds, or until golden. Add a splash of water to the pan and cover with the lid. Cook for a further 1–2 minutes, or until the cheese is melted. Repeat to cook the remaining sandwich.

Top each tuna melt with a pickled pepper and cut in half to serve.

CLASSIC GREEK SALAD (V)

Time
15 minutes

SERVES 4 (AS A SIDE)

1 red onion
2 garlic cloves
½ lemon
1 tablespoon white vinegar
1 tablespoon dried oregano
2 Lebanese (short) cucumbers
3 tomatoes
20 pitted kalamata olives
2 tablespoons extra-virgin olive oil
Salt and cracked black pepper, to taste
200 g (7 oz) piece feta cheese (see Notes)
Fresh bread, to serve (optional)

Notes

- To make this salad vegan, omit the feta.
- Feel free to halve the amount of cheese. I have just kept this as traditional as possible – and the Greeks do love to chuck a whole block on top!

More commonly known as horiatiki salata in Greece – meaning village salad – this is what the world knows as Greek salad. Greece has a myriad of salads, but every menu throughout Greece will feature this combination of ingredients. The islands among the Cyclades will sometimes add capers and green capsicum (pepper), but this version is the salad I grew up eating. Its origins come from farmers putting together any vegetables they had on hand and dressing them with oil and lemon. It's now become a fully developed recipe that transports you to Greece with every bite. Make sure to eat it like a Greek: with a bit of fresh bread to dip into the dressing.

Thinly slice the onion and mince the garlic, and transfer both to a large bowl. Finely grate in the zest of the lemon half, then squeeze in the juice. Add the vinegar, half the oregano, a big pinch of salt and a few cracks of pepper to the bowl. Mix everything together. Set aside while you prep the rest of the ingredients to mellow out the harshness of the raw onion.

Cut the cucumbers in half lengthways, then slice into half-moon pieces. Cut each tomato into eight wedges, then in half crossways, so you have bite-sized chunks.

Add the tomato, cucumber, olives and oil to the onion mixture and toss together. Season with salt. Transfer the salad to a serving bowl, then top with the whole piece of feta and sprinkle with the remaining oregano. To serve, break the feta into the salad and enjoy it all together with bread, if using.

GREEK GODDESS DRESSING (VE)

Time
15 minutes

MAKES ENOUGH TO DRESS 1 LARGE SALAD

1 large bunch fresh oregano
1 large bunch fresh tarragon
4 garlic cloves
1 lemon
2 tablespoons extra-virgin olive oil, plus extra if needed
2 heaped tablespoons hulled tahini
Salt, to taste

Notes

- If the dressing is too thick, add a little more olive oil and blend to your desired consistency.
- This dressing makes enough for 1 large salad. For a smaller salad, either halve the quantities or make as above and store the remainder in the fridge for up to 3 days.

Green goddess dressing had me in a stranglehold for most of 2023, and for good reason. There are a million different variations out there on the internet, but this is the one I tend to make the most, just because of what herbs I have in my fridge. The tarragon adds a lovely floral, aniseed note, the oregano an earthy bitterness and the lemon a vibrant acidity. There's a gentle burn from the garlic, then a massive nutty hit from the tahini. Feel free to swap herbs, like mint, basil, parsley or even some baby spinach. It can really be a choose-your-own-adventure, but this is my Greek version that I live by. It works particularly well on cabbage-based slaws.

Pick all the oregano and tarragon leaves, and place them in a food processor. Roughly chop the garlic and add to the processor. Halve the lemon and squeeze in the juice of both halves. Add the oil, tahini and a pinch of salt. Process until smooth and a thick dressing consistency (see Notes). Adjust seasoning with salt, then do a final blitz.

Left to right: Classic salad dressing (page 50), Honey mustard Greek yoghurt dressing (page 51) and Greek goddess dressing (opposite).

CLASSIC SALAD DRESSING (VE)

Time
5 minutes

MAKES ENOUGH TO DRESS 1 LARGE SALAD

½ lemon
¼ cup (60 ml) extra-virgin olive oil
1 tablespoon red wine vinegar
Salt, to taste

Note
This dressing makes enough for 1 large salad. For a smaller salad, either halve the quantities or make as above and store the remainder in the fridge for up to 4 days.

This dressing is a simple approach to bringing fat, acid and salt together. It's an all-rounder that works with leafy salads, tomato salads and everything in between. Add a minced garlic clove for a bit of spice or enjoy as is.

Squeeze the juice of the lemon half into a small jar. Add the oil and vinegar. Seal and shake until well combined. Season with salt.

HONEY MUSTARD GREEK YOGHURT DRESSING (V)

Time
10 minutes

MAKES ENOUGH TO DRESS 1 LARGE SALAD

1 garlic clove
1 tablespoon extra-virgin olive oil
1 tablespoon Dijon mustard
1 tablespoon honey
3–4 tablespoons Greek-style yoghurt
Salt, to taste

Note
This dressing makes enough for 1 large salad. For a smaller salad, either halve the quantities or make as above and store the remainder in the fridge for up to 1 week.

This is a punchy little dressing that works incredibly well with leafy green salads. It takes just minutes to make and elevates any salad instantly. If you like it punchier, reduce the amount of Greek yoghurt, or alternatively, increase the amount for a more delicate dressing. My favourite way to have it is on a wedge of iceberg, topped with grated kefalotyri.

Roughly chop the garlic, then transfer it to a jar or beaker, along with the oil, mustard, honey and 3 tablespoons yoghurt. Using a hand-held blender, blend until smooth. Season with salt and blend again. Taste and add the remaining yoghurt for a milder flavour, if you like (but keep in mind that once tossed with a salad, it will also become milder).

LETTUCE SALAD (V)

MAROULOSALATA

Time
15 minutes

SERVES 4–6 (AS A SIDE)

1 bunch spring onions (scallions)
3 garlic cloves
1 lemon
1 tablespoon white vinegar
2 teaspoons salt, plus extra to taste
40 g (1½ oz) fresh dill
1 iceberg lettuce
⅓ cup (80 ml) extra-virgin olive oil
1 tablespoon dried oregano
200 g (7 oz) feta cheese

This simple salad has changed my life in many ways. This was my first viral video on social media, with over 16 million views. It took my working career as a content creator to another level. I am so glad it was a salad I grew up eating. My yiayia served it with every meal, hers dripping with dressing; it was closer to a dressing soup with floating lettuce! I've fine-tuned the recipe a little bit so it still has that glistening dressing all over, but you're not drinking it. Now, to the Greek purists, yes, technically it should be made with cos lettuce – not iceberg – and no feta, but this is how Yiayia Maria made it, and I think it's perfect! Feel free to swap out the lettuce if it makes you feel better.

Thinly slice the spring onions and mince the garlic, and place both in a large salad bowl. Finely grate in the zest of the lemon, then halve the lemon and squeeze in the juice of both halves. Add the vinegar and salt. Mix together and set aside while you prep the dill and lettuce to mellow out the harshness of the raw onion and garlic.

Finely chop the dill and thinly shred the lettuce.

Add the oil, oregano and dill to the bowl and mix through. In batches, toss the lettuce in the bowl, rolling it through the dressing until well coated. Finally, crumble in the feta and mix through. Season with extra salt if needed. (You want the salad to be really zesty and bright so it can accompany fatty and heavier proteins.)

CITRUS HERBED RICE (VE)

Time
30 minutes

SERVES 4 (AS A SIDE)

2 tablespoons olive oil
1 brown onion
300 g (10½ oz) long-grain white rice
650 ml (22½ fl oz) vegetable stock (see Note)
1 orange
1 lemon
30 g (1 oz) fresh flat-leaf (Italian) parsley sprigs
30 g (1 oz) fresh dill
Salt, to taste

Note
If it's not important for the dish to be vegan, you can use chicken stock instead.

A simple side rice is delicious, but this citrus and herb, almost pilaf-style rice is the only way to go. It really gives the rice main-character energy. The citrus and herbs make this a dish in itself, but it also goes so well with any protein. Feel free to swap in whatever citrus and herbs you have, or whatever is in season.

Heat a saucepan over medium–low heat, then add half the oil. Roughly chop the onion, then add to the pan with a pinch of salt and cook, stirring, for 2 minutes, or until softened. Add the rice and cook, stirring, for 1 minute, or until translucent. Pour in the stock. Stir, scraping the base of the pan. Increase heat to medium and bring to the boil. Cover and cook, stirring occasionally, for 14–15 minutes, or until al dente. Take off the heat.

Meanwhile, finely grate the orange and lemon zest into a bowl. Halve the lemon and squeeze in the juice of 1 half. Add the remaining 1 tablespoon oil and a pinch of salt, and mix together. Pick the parsley leaves, then finely chop, along with the dill.

Add the oil mixture and herbs to the rice and mix together. Cover with the lid and set aside for 5 minutes, or until the rice is fluffy.

Squeeze in the juice of the remaining lemon half, mix through and season with salt to serve.

WATERMELON, FETA AND MINT

Time
25 minutes

SERVES 6
(AS A SIDE)

¼ small watermelon
100 g (3½ oz) prosciutto
100 g (3½ oz) feta cheese
Cracked black pepper, to taste

MINT SALSA VERDE
1 bunch fresh flat-leaf (Italian) parsley
1 bunch fresh mint
1 lemon
3 garlic cloves
2 anchovies
100 ml (3½ fl oz) extra-virgin olive oil
Salt, to taste

Notes

- To make this salad vegetarian, omit the prosciutto and swap the anchovies in the salsa verde for capers.
- The mint salsa verde will keep in an airtight container in the fridge for up to 3 days.

There are a million and one variations of the watermelon, feta and mint salad, so here's another one to add to the list. I find whole pieces of mint to be a bit full-on, depending on which part of the salad you're eating, so I make a mint salsa verde as the dressing. This spreads the mint flavour nicely amongst it all. The addition of prosciutto is inspired by the Spaniards adding jamon to rockmelon – one of my favourite small plates. It gives the whole dish some wonderful fattiness and creaminess that ties all the elements together.

To make the mint salsa verde, pick the parsley and mint leaves, and add to a food processor. Finely grate in the zest of the lemon. Halve the lemon and squeeze in the juice of both halves. Roughly chop the garlic, then add to the processor, along with the anchovies. Blend until smooth. With the motor running, slowly pour in the oil until a pesto-like consistency. Season with salt. Place in the fridge until required.

Peel and chop the watermelon into 2 cm (¾ in) cubes and arrange on a serving platter. Arrange the prosciutto between the watermelon chunks so it pokes out like little flowers. Crumble the feta over the top. Spoon the mint salsa verde over the salad. Season with pepper.

Time
15 minutes

CRETAN RUSK TOMATO SALAD (V)

SERVES 2
(AS A SIDE)

DAKOS

4 barley rusks (see Notes)
3 large tomatoes
2 tablespoons extra-virgin olive oil
15 pitted kalamata olives
2 tablespoons baby capers
2 teaspoons red wine vinegar
80 g (2¾ oz) feta cheese, crumbled
Salt and cracked black pepper, to taste
2 teaspoons dried oregano

Notes

- To make this salad vegan, omit the feta.
- Cretan barley rusks are hard to source unless you are in Greece or have a local Greek or specialty Mediterranean grocer nearby. They are twice-cooked, incredibly hard and need to be softened before eating. Major supermarkets have different rusk varieties, such as Dutch rusks, so if you need to use those, you may not need to do the dipping process. Test before doing the whole batch, as they may fall apart. If you can't find any rusks, use day-old bread cut into large cubes, drizzled with oil and toasted in the oven like large croutons. Spoon the bread over the salad to serve.

The year was 2012 and I ventured to the Greek Islands for the first time. I sat down in a restaurant on the island of Ios with my mate and ordered a selection of plates. After eating a Greek salad every day for a week, we thought we'd try dakos salad – a Cretan salad using old barley rusks, topped with tomato and feta. I can still remember the juicy tomatoes exploding over the crunchy rusks and the tangy feta cutting through it all – I have been in love with it ever since. Because of this salad's simplicity, using high-quality tomatoes is essential. It's worth waiting until they're in season to whip up this plate.

Fill a large bowl with water. Dip the barley rusks in the water for a second, then pull them out. Shake off the excess water and place on a large serving plate. Discard the water.

Coarsely grate 1 tomato, discarding the skin, then add to the same bowl used for the rusks, along with half the oil and a pinch of salt. Mix together, then spoon onto the rusks.

Finely chop the remaining tomatoes, roughly chop the olives and capers, and add it all to the bowl. Add the vinegar, a few cracks of pepper and a pinch of salt, and mix together. Spoon the mixture over the rusks. Crumble the feta over, then top with the oregano and remaining 1 tablespoon oil.

SIMPLE FISH

Time
20 minutes

SERVES 2 (AS A SHARED PLATE)

2 garlic cloves
10 g (⅓ oz) fresh flat-leaf (Italian) parsley leaves
1 lemon
¼ cup (35 g) plain (all-purpose) flour
1 tablespoon olive oil
1 thin white fish fillet
20 g (¾ oz) butter
Salt, to taste

When I think of the Greek Islands, my brain immediately goes to simple seafood cooked well – nothing fancy, just delicious white fish with lots of lemon. This is my take on both that taste and carefree island eating. Warning: I use butter. I know, it's not very Greek, but the butter makes the sauce that you pour over the fish with the lemon, garlic and parsley. It's really special, considering how quick it is to make. Once you've got the hang of my simple fish, it will very quickly make its way into your weeknight cooking. Plus, thinner white fish fillets tend to be on the cheaper side, meaning it won't cost a bomb to enjoy such a special plate.

Thinly slice the garlic, pick and finely chop the parsley leaves and halve the lemon ready to juice. Spread the flour over a large plate. Grab the fish and season with a pinch of salt on both sides, then pat in the flour on both sides. Shake off any excess flour.

Heat a large frying pan over high heat, then pour in the oil. Add the fish and cook for 3 minutes (you want a nice golden char). Turn and cook on the other side for a further 3 minutes. Reduce heat to low and add the butter, garlic and juice from 1 lemon half. Once the butter melts, spoon the mixture over the fish to baste for 1 minute. Take off the heat and transfer the fish to a serving plate. Juice the remaining lemon half into the pan. Sprinkle with the parsley and a pinch of salt.

Pour the sauce over the fish to serve.

PASTA IN VERDE SAUCE

Time
20 minutes

SERVES 2

SALMORIGLIO HILOPITES

4 garlic cloves
1 bunch fresh oregano
1 lemon
3 anchovies
Extra-virgin olive oil
200 g (7 oz) hilopites pasta (see Note)
Salt and cracked black pepper, to taste
50 g (1¾ oz) feta cheese

Note
Make your own Fresh pasta (page 141) or use store-bought dried hilopites and follow packet directions to cook.

A quick pasta is a staple for me, particularly when it's as punchy and zingy as this one, singing from the combination of herbs and citrus. This is a dish that helped my team win a pasta challenge on *MasterChef*, and I used it because I was able to get the salmoriglio sauce done so quickly. The verde sauce (salmoriglio), from Southern Italy, is wonderfully versatile. You can enjoy it tossed through pasta, dolloped onto grilled fish or mixed through deeply charred vegetables. The dish I presented on *MasterChef* used fried capers for texture and crunch, so I recommend frying some up and scattering them over the pasta, if you have time.

Roughly chop the garlic and pick the oregano leaves. Add both to a mortar. Halve the lemon and squeeze in the juice of both halves. Add the anchovies and enough oil to cover all the ingredients, then pound with the pestle until the mixture breaks down into a very green sauce. Season with salt and pepper. (Alternatively, add all the ingredients to a food processor and blitz until smooth and bright green, adding oil as needed until a smooth saucy consistency.)

Bring a saucepan of salted water to the boil over high heat. Add the pasta and cook for 1 minutes 30 seconds, or until al dente. Drain. Transfer to a large serving bowl. Add the salmoriglio and stir until well combined.

Finely grate the feta over to serve.

Time
25 minutes

GARLIC AND TOMATO PASTA (VE)

SERVES 2

SKORDOMAKARONA

6 garlic cloves
2 large ripe tomatoes
250 g (9 oz) dried spaghetti (see Note)
¼ cup (60 ml) olive oil
30 g (1 oz) fresh flat-leaf (Italian) parsley leaves
Salt and cracked black pepper, to taste
20 g (¾ oz) barley rusk (see Notes)

Notes

- To make this pasta vegan, use pasta that is egg free.
- You can buy barley rusks at the supermarket.

A simple pasta recipe that can be whipped up when the fridge is empty is always appreciated. Skordomakarona stems from poorer times in Greece. It's simple and relies on the marriage between garlic, oil and tomato. It all comes together really quickly. When you eat and serve it, you'll be shocked at the flavour you've achieved in such a short time. If you can, don't skip the rusk on top. It's what makes this dish so iconic. The crumbles of rusk create this meaty, mince-like texture that become little flavour bombs as they soak up all the sauce.

Bring a large saucepan of salted boiling water to the boil over high heat.

While the water comes to the boil, begin the sauce. Thinly slice the garlic and coarsely grate the tomatoes into a bowl, discarding the skin.

Cook the pasta in the pan following packet directions until al dente. Drain, reserving ¾ cup (185 ml) pasta water.

Meanwhile, heat a frying pan over medium–low heat, then pour in the oil. Add the garlic, a pinch of salt and a few cracks of pepper. Cook, stirring constantly, for 5 minutes, or until the garlic has softened (but not crisped up). Mix through the tomato. Increase heat to medium and let it bubble away for 10 minutes. Season with salt.

Add the pasta and reserved pasta water to the tomato mixture and cook, stirring, over medium heat for 1 minute to bring everything together. Take off the heat.

Roughly chop the parsley, then stir it through the pasta. Plate up, then crumble the rusk over to serve.

CRUSTACEAN PASTA

ASTAKOMAKARONADA

Time
30 minutes

SERVES 2

2 large tomatoes
2 × 200 g (7 oz) Moreton bay bugs (see Notes)
200 g (7 oz) dried spaghetti
2 tablespoons olive oil
1 large French shallot
4 garlic cloves
70 g (2½ oz) tomato paste (concentrated purée)
1½ cups (375 ml) chicken stock
Salt and cracked black pepper, to taste
1 small bunch fresh oregano
1½ tablespoons baby capers
½ lemon

Notes

- If Moreton bay bugs aren't available, lobster, crayfish, langoustines or even large tiger prawns will work instead. Adjust the cooking time for the substituted crustacean and continue with the recipe as is.
- If increasing the recipe quantity, add an additional Moreton Bay bug per serving.

TASTES EVEN BETTER THE NEXT DAY

I've done a series called PASTABOIS with my best mate Max. We met at the *MasterChef* auditions. From that moment we've been mates. He taught me everything about pasta, so when I left the show, we decided to film pasta recipes together. It became a reason to hang out, drink wine and cook together, but it's also my favourite content to make. When I asked Max to create a recipe for the book to represent PASTABOIS, his take on astakomakaronada surpassed my expectations. This dish is traditionally a lobster spaghetti, cooked in island tavernas. It's so delicious considering how quickly it comes together. Max uses Moreton Bay bugs to keep it affordable, but pick any crustacean you like or what's available.

Bring a large saucepan of salted water to the boil over high heat. Score a cross in the top of each tomato with a small, sharp knife, then add to the pan. Cook for 45 seconds, or until the skin begins to peel away. Take off the heat. Using a slotted spoon, transfer tomatoes to a chopping board, reserving the water in the pan. When cool enough to handle, peel off the skin, deseed and dice.

Return the pan of reserved water to the boil over high heat. Set up an ice bath in a large bowl. Add the bugs to the pan and cook for 4–5 minutes, or until the shells turn reddish orange (make sure the water stays at a rolling boil the whole time). Transfer the bugs to the ice bath until cooled completely.

Using a sharp knife, pierce the middle of each bug, then cut down hard along the length. Remove the poop shoot, then set aside the bug halves.

Discard water from pan and refill with fresh water. Season with salt and bring to the boil over high heat. Cook the pasta following packet directions until just before al dente. Drain, reserving ½ cup (125 ml) pasta water.

Meanwhile, heat the oil in a large frying pan over medium heat. Finely chop the shallot. Add to the pan with a pinch of salt. Cook, stirring, for 2 minutes to soften. Mince the garlic and add to the pan with a splash of water. Cook for 1 minute, or until fragrant. Stir in the tomato paste for 1 minute. Add the stock. Bring to the boil, then cook for 1 minute. Add the bugs, stirring to coat in the sauce.

Add the pasta and half the reserved pasta water. Stir until combined. Add a little more pasta water to loosen the sauce if needed. Stir for 30 seconds to warm through.

Pick the oregano leaves and add to the pasta, along with the capers and diced tomato. Season. Cut the lemon half into wedges to squeeze over everything.

CALAMARI WITH SUPERCHARGED TARTARE

Time
30 minutes

SERVES 4

2 squid tubes
1 teaspoon caster (superfine) sugar
8 cups (2 litres) canola oil
⅔ cup (100 g) plain (all-purpose) flour
⅓ cup (65 g) fine semolina
⅓ cup (40 g) cornflour (corn starch)
Salt and cracked black pepper, to taste
Lemon wedges, to serve

SUPERCHARGED TARTARE
30 g (1 oz) fresh flat-leaf (Italian) parsley sprigs
30 g (1 oz) fresh dill
½ French shallot
1 dill pickle
1 tablespoon baby capers
½ lemon
100 g (3½ oz) mayonnaise
Salt, to taste

Note
If you don't have a cook's thermometer to test when the oil is ready, put the handle end of a wooden spoon in the oil. If tiny bubbles gather around the handle, the oil is ready.

The Greek Islands are known for their seafood, specifically squid, which is an integral part of every island diet. There are a lot of ways to cook squid, from stuffing it for the dish kalamaria gemista, to simply grilling it on the barbecue with lots of lemon. Calamari is always a wonderful way to showcase the protein squid, and the way I make it is heavily inspired by the way the Greek Islands coat and cook it. The coating is made with semolina for texture and cornflour (corn starch) for crunch. Most importantly, it gets coated twice, with a dunk in ice-cold water in between, which Greeks swear gives it a wonderful crunchy finish. I very much agree. If you've ever struggled with calamari, this recipe is for you, because the coating always sticks and comes up crunchy. Aim for a 45-second cook for the most tender squid.

Slice the squid into strips, cutting against the grain so you end up with 1–2 cm (½–¾ in) wide rings. Place in a bowl, along with the sugar. Season with salt and pepper, then massage into the squid. Set aside to allow the sugar to tenderise the squid while you make the tartare.

To make the supercharged tartare, pick the parsley leaves and remove any thick stems from the dill. Finely chop the herbs and place in a bowl. Finely chop the shallot, pickle and capers, and add to the bowl. Squeeze in the juice of the lemon half. Add the mayonnaise and mix together. Season with salt. Place in the fridge until required.

Pour the oil into a deep medium saucepan. Heat over high heat until the temperature reaches 180°C (350°F) on a cook's thermometer (see Note).

Place the flour, semolina, cornflour and 2 pinches of salt in a large bowl and mix together. Fill a separate large bowl with ice-cold water and place next to the bowl of flour mixture. Line a plate with paper towel. (This is to drain the calamari after frying.)

Place half the squid in the flour mixture and toss to coat evenly, shaking off any excess. Dunk in the ice-cold water, then return to the flour mixture to coat evenly again. Carefully place in the hot oil and fry for 45 seconds (or no longer than 1 minute). Using a slotted spoon, transfer to the prepared plate. Repeat the process with the remaining squid.

Serve with lemon wedges and the tartare on the side.

CHOCOLATE AND FETA STUFFED DATES

Time
25 minutes

MAKES 12–15

1 orange
200 g (7 oz) feta cheese
2 tablespoons sesame seeds
100 g (3½ oz) dark chocolate (70% cocoa) melts
200 g (7 oz) medjool dates
Flaky sea salt, to taste

Note
If the whipped feta gets too wet, simply transfer the mixture to a small tray, spreading over the base. Place the open and deseeded dates on top, pushing them into the whipped feta. Top with the chocolate, toasted sesame seeds and sea salt, and place in the fridge to firm up a bit. Scoop out a date and some whipped feta whenever you want one.

When it comes to fast little sweet treats, medjool dates are always a favourite. Filled with zesty, whipped feta cheese and topped with dark chocolate and a pinch of flaky salt, these two or three biters are wonderfully sweet and balanced with just the right amount of savoury. Plus, the addition of lightly toasted sesame seeds sprinkled over gives these stuffed dates a nutty crunch that ties everything together. If you've ever had a feta-based cheesecake, you'll know how wonderful this cheese is when it comes to incorporating it into desserts.

Finely grate the zest of the orange into a food processor. Add the feta, then blitz on high. Next, you need to add the orange juice. As the size of each orange varies, the amount of juice will also vary depending on how big the fruit is. Quarter the orange and gradually squeeze in no more than a quarter of the orange juice, adding just small squeezes as you process until the mixture is homogenous, making sure the whipped feta doesn't get too wet. Give the processor time to blitz as well; the longer the mixture is processing, the smoother it'll get naturally. You want a firm texture that holds its shape – not the texture of a dip. Once it's ready, place the processor bowl, with the lid still on, in the fridge until ready to use. If the whipped feta gets too wet and resembles more of a dip texture as you're adding orange juice, don't stress, these things happen to the best of us. See the Note on how to salvage the whipped feta mixture by turning it into a tray dessert.

Place the sesame seeds in a small dry saucepan over medium heat. Once the pan heats up, swirl the pan until the sesame seeds are toasted light brown. (Swirling the pan frequently helps make sure the sesame seeds don't burn as they toast.)

Place the dark chocolate melts in a small microwave-safe bowl. Microwave for 20-second intervals, stirring in between interval, until the chocolate is melted and a pourable consistency. (This shouldn't take any longer than 90 seconds.)

Set a large wire rack over a piece of baking paper or a tray. Using a sharp knife, cut open the dates lengthways down one side (just enough to open up, not all the way through). Remove the seeds and the hard crowns. Using a small spoon, stuff some of the whipped feta into the cut of each date. Place the stuffed dates on the wire rack. Spoon the melted chocolate over one end of each date, then sprinkle with the toasted sesame seeds and a pinch of flaky sea salt. Enjoy the delicious stuffed dates immediately or store them in an airtight container in the fridge to eat later on – they will keep for up to a week.

ROASTED HONEY PEACHES

Time
30 minutes

SERVES 2

4 ripe yellow peaches
1 lemon
10 g (⅓ oz) fresh rosemary sprigs
150 g (5½ oz) honey
¾ cup (200 g) Greek-style yoghurt
Salt, to taste

Notes

- If you're not eating the roasted peaches all at once, store them, submerged in the syrup, in the fridge for up to 5 days. The syrup will continue to infuse the peaches as time goes on.
- The syrup also works incredibly well in cocktails, so make sure to store in a sterilised airtight container in the fridge for up to 6 months for happy hour at your house.

TASTES EVEN BETTER THE NEXT DAY

Juicy peaches remind me of Greece more than any fruit. Picking up some from a little fruit shop on the way to the beach, then enjoying them as the juices run down your hand and mouth, making everything slightly sticky – it's Greek summer in a nutshell. These quick roasted peaches seem deceptively simple, because they are, but the result is a wonderful combination of lemon, honey and rosemary. Sometimes really good ingredients don't need a lot done to them. Great for breakfast with granola, or as a simple dessert number, they're versatile and wildly delicious.

Preheat oven to 180°C (350°F) fan-forced.

Cut the peaches into quarters and remove the pits. Transfer the peach quarters to a small, deep baking tray, arranging them so they fit snugly.

Zest the lemon into a bowl, then halve the lemon and squeeze in the juice of 1 half. Pick the rosemary leaves and add to the bowl, along with 100 g (3½ oz) honey and a pinch of salt. Mix together.

Pour the lemon mixture over the fruit and mix all together until coated. Arrange the peach quarters cut-side up with the skin in the syrup. Roast for 20 minutes, or until a spoon easily cuts through the fruit.

While the peaches roast, place the yoghurt and remaining 50 g (1¾ oz) honey in a bowl and whisk together until smooth. Place in the fridge until ready to serve.

Transfer the roasted peaches to serving bowls, top with some of the syrup from the tray and finish with the sweetened yoghurt on top (see Notes).

Time
30 minutes

CHERRY ETON MESS

SERVES 4

KERASI MESS

500 g (1 lb 2 oz) frozen pitted cherries
1 cup (220 g) caster (superfine) sugar
80 g (2¾ oz) store-bought meringue nests

CHANTILLY CREAM
300 ml (10½ fl oz) thickened (whipping) cream
250 g (9 oz) mascarpone
¼ cup (30 g) icing (confectioners') sugar
1 tablespoon vanilla extract

Note
You can prep all the elements early on, so it's just an assembly job when you're ready to serve. Cook the cherry syrup up to 24 hours ahead and store in the fridge. Whip with the Chantilly cream up to a day ahead, cover the bowl with plastic wrap and store in the fridge to keep stable. Pre-crush the meringues and pop them in an airtight container at room temperature. Build the mess in the glasses right before serving.

A lot of Greek desserts take time. They're a labour of love, and while that is wonderful, sometimes you just want a show-stopping dessert that's quick. My kerasi mess is a crowd-pleaser, which pays homage to the history of glyko, in particular glyko kerasi. Greek glykos are spoon sweets: bite-sized fruits, cooked in sugar to become little sweet bites to eat after dinner. They're often made with waste products, like orange peel, watermelon skin and unripe walnuts. This mess is layered with a quick, vanilla-hit Chantilly cream, crunchy meringue pieces and sweet, syrupy cherries that are often the nostalgic star of Greek spoon sweets.

Place a heatproof bowl in the freezer to chill while you make the dessert.

Place the cherries and caster sugar in saucepan over medium heat. Cook until the sugar dissolves, then bring to a simmer, reduce heat to low and gently simmer for 12–15 minutes. (You want the cherries to soften and release their liquid to create a syrupy consistency.) Pour the mixture into the chilled bowl and place in the freezer for 5 minutes to chill.

While the cherries cook, make the Chantilly cream. Place all the ingredients in a stand mixer with the whisk attachment. Whisk on low speed until soft peaks form. (Don't over-whisk or the cream will separate; just enough that it holds its shape when the whisk is pulled out.) Place in the fridge until ready to serve.

Grab four large serving glasses and spoon in a layer of Chantilly cream, crumble in some meringue, then top with some cherries in the syrup. Continue layering until each glass is filled so you have multiple layers.

QUICK COCKTAILS

SANTORINI SOUR

Time
10 minutes

SERVES 1

45 ml (1½ fl oz) gin
20 ml (½ fl oz) Italicus Rosolio di Bergamotto liqueur (see Notes)
20 ml (½ fl oz) blue Curaçao liqueur
30 ml (1 fl oz) fresh lemon juice
1 egg white
Ice cubes
Bitters, for garnishing

Notes

- To make this cocktail vegan, substitute the egg white for 30 ml (1 fl oz) aquafaba (the liquid from tinned chickpeas).
- Italicus Rosolio di Bergamotto liqueur is a fragrant, herb-focused aperitivo. Find it at selected bottle shops.

A drink that resembles the coastline of Santorini is a must for any Greek dinner party. Sours are one of my favourite cocktail styles, as they bring a creamy elegance to the drinks world. The deep blue bottom of this drink represents the ocean surrounding Santorini's coast, and the foamy top is the white houses that adorn the mountains. The flavour is tart, but light, with a lovely dryness, which feels like you're drinking it in a beachside taverna off a Greek island. This sour is a loose take on the Italian classic, Angelo Azzurro, which was a beloved cocktail from the 1990s, and named after a gay bar in Rome. Any drink that brings my community together is one I can get around, and I really enjoy this more approachable take compared to the incredibly boozy original.

Place a coupe glass in the freezer to chill while you make the cocktail.

Place the gin, liqueurs, lemon juice and egg white in a cocktail shaker. Shake dry for 15 seconds, or until combined. Add ice cubes to the shaker and shake vigorously for 15 seconds, or until the shaker is frosted.

Double strain the sour into the chilled glass. Decorate with 3 drops of bitters. Using a toothpick, drag the bitters through the foam to create lovely little heart shapes.

CINNAMON SYRUP (VE)

KANELADA

Time
30 minutes

MAKES 1 CUP (250 ML)

1 cup (220 g) caster (superfine) sugar
6 cinnamon sticks
6 whole cloves
½ lemon
2–3 drops red liquid food colouring

Note
This syrup will keep in the fridge for up to 6 months, ready to go for drinks or cocktails.

Kanelada is a traditional Cretan cordial used to add flavour to water and ice. It's sometimes stirred through boiling water and sipped slowly, like a tea. As you read this book, you'll start to notice Greeks love syrup, and this is one of my favourites, because it gives me that nostalgic Greek hit. The flavours are similar to the cinnamon lollies left on every yiayia's table (the Greeks will know what I am talking about). I like to use this syrup to level up classic cocktails (like my Kanelada hot toddy on page 80 and Kanelada negroni, opposite), or to flavour freshly bubbled soda water (club soda). You will very rarely see me use food colouring in my cooking, but it's necessary for the kanelada. This syrup is traditionally red because it's made with flowers, like carnations, which give it a deep red hue. They are a bit hard to come by, so a couple drops of red food colouring do the trick. You can always omit and just enjoy the golden, straw colour it gets from the woody spices.

Place the sugar, cinnamon, cloves and 2 cups (500 ml) water in a small saucepan over medium heat. Bring to the boil, then reduce heat to low and gently simmer for 15 minutes, or until the syrup tastes spice heavy. Take off the heat.

Squeeze the juice of the lemon half into the pan. Add the colouring and stir until well combined.

If using immediately, strain through a sieve, discarding the solids.

If not using immediately, transfer to a sterilised, heatproof and airtight container and set aside to cool completely (for how to sterilise, see Notes page 39). Place in the fridge overnight.

The next day, strain the syrup through a sieve, discarding the solids.

KANELADA NEGRONI (VE)

Time
5 minutes

SERVES 1

30 ml (1 fl oz) gin
30 ml (1 fl oz) Campari
22.5 ml (¾ fl oz) Cinnamon syrup (opposite)
Ice cubes, plus 1 large ice cube to serve (see Note)
Orange wedge, to serve

Note
If you don't have a large ice cube tray, you can use a few regular ice cubes to serve instead.

Of all the cocktails you can make with cinnamon syrup, this is the one for slow sipping. I love a negroni, and this version just makes a lot of sense. Swap the sweet vermouth for a smaller amount of the syrup and the result is so beautifully cohesive. The botanical gin with the bitter orange of Campari pairs really well with the cinnamon-focused kanelada. The result has a natural smoky tone that allows the bitterness (which I love) to meld into a lasting cinnamon finish. Play around with the ratios if you prefer it sweeter, and remember: it's easy to prep a batch ahead and store in the fridge, ready for when mates come over.

Place the gin, Campari and cinnamon syrup in a cocktail mixing jug, cocktail shaker or pint glass and fill with ice cubes. Stir for 30 seconds, or until well combined and the glass is frosted.

Place the large ice cube in a rocks glass. Strain the negroni over the ice. Finish with the orange wedge in between the glass and ice to serve.

ORANGE AND FENNEL MARGARITA (VE)

Time
15 minutes

SERVES 1

2 teaspoons dried fennel seeds
1 tablespoon flaky sea salt
30 ml (1 fl oz) tequila blanco
30 ml (1 fl oz) mastiha (see Note)
20 ml (½ fl oz) fresh orange juice, plus extra wedge for garnishing
20 ml (½ fl oz) fresh lime juice, reserving the juiced lime to rim the glass
10 ml (¼ fl oz) agave
Ice cubes

Note
Find mastiha at selected bottle shops.

The marg is iconic; it is the moment, it is a vibe, it is everything when it comes to having a cocktail with mates, sun glaring down and nothing to worry about except reapplying your sunscreen. So, why shouldn't the margarita get the Greek treatment? The combination of orange, fennel and mastiha creates the margarita you never knew you needed. It's crunchy and zingy, like a classic marg, but made a lot more interesting. It'll make you look at your mate and smile after every sip. Mastiha and agave both come from plants and are a really underrated combination, particularly when you add tequila to the mix. This drink feels savoury and herbaceous without losing the elements of a classic margarita.

Heat a frying pan over medium heat. Add the fennel seeds and cook, stirring, until lightly browned and fragrant. Transfer to a mortar and use a pestle to break down the seeds. Add the salt. Gently mix together with a spoon. Spread the mixture over a plate.

Pour the tequila, mastiha, orange juice, lime juice and agave into a cocktail shaker and fill with ice cubes. Shake for 15 seconds, or until well combined.

Rim the side of a medium rocks glass with the reserved lime half, then dip in the fennel mixture to coat.

Double strain the margarita into the prepared glass. Top up with fresh ice cubes. Finish with an orange wedge to serve. Enjoy the drink with little bits of fennel salt as you sip.

KANELADA HOT TODDY (VE)

Time
5 minutes

SERVES 1

15 ml (½ fl oz) fresh lemon juice, plus extra lemon slice (optional) for garnishing
30 ml (1 fl oz) Cinnamon syrup (page 76)
150 ml (5 fl oz) boiling water
60 ml (2 fl oz) whiskey

In the depths of winter, I want nothing more than to sit on the couch with a loved one (or preferably by myself) and watch a movie with a warming drink in hand. If that's you too, look no further than this hot toddy. The best part is the cinnamon syrup – it's all cloves and cinnamon, so is already giving you the woody spice notes that a hot toddy loves. The smokiness of the whiskey pairs with the sharpness and brightness of the lemon. Mixed with the spice-driven sweetness of the syrup, it's all warmed together to make this the best fireplace treat.

Place the lemon juice, cinnamon syrup and boiling water in a heatproof cup or mug. Give it a quick stir, then add the whiskey.

Top with a lemon slice, if using.

CUCUMBER AND OREGANO GIMLET (VE)

Time
5 minutes

SERVES 1

4 fresh oregano sprigs
3 thin Lebanese (short) cucumber slices
15 ml (½ fl oz) Simple sugar syrup (page 16)
60 ml (2 fl oz) gin
30 ml (1 fl oz) fresh lime juice
Ice cubes
Extra-virgin olive oil, to serve

Originally created to cure scurvy, the gimlet is one of the oldest cocktails in history, and stands the test of time because of its simplicity. Traditionally made with rose lime cordial, today it features a mixture of fresh lime and cordial to complement the botanical gin. My more Greek take brings together earthy, slightly bitter oregano and a crisp, sweet freshness from the cucumber to create a savoury, springtime note for an afternoon tipple in the sun.

Place a coupe glass in the freezer to chill while you make the cocktail.

Pick the leaves from 3 oregano sprigs. Add to a cocktail shaker, along with the cucumber and sugar syrup. Using a muddler or the end of a wooden spoon, muddle the mixture until fragrant and broken down well. Pour in the gin and lime juice. Fill with ice cubes and shake hard for 15 seconds, or until the shaker is frosted.

Double strain the gimlet into the chilled glass. Decorate with 3 drops of oil and the remaining oregano sprig to serve.

ESPRESSO MARTINI FRAPPE

Time
10 minutes

SERVES 1

1 tablespoon instant coffee granules
20 ml (½ fl oz) vodka
15 ml (½ fl oz) Kahlúa coffee liqueur
10 ml (¼ fl oz) Simple sugar syrup (page 16)
Ice cubes

Note
If you prefer a sweeter frappe, add a dash more sugar syrup, then froth until the frappe comes three-quarters of the way up the glass.

One of life's simplest pleasures is sitting on a balcony, listening to the sounds of the city, sipping your frappe. No matter how you take yours (I'm a little sugar but no milk), it always hits the spot. So, it made sense to turn the humble day drink into a night-time espresso martini, considering both drinks are beloved for their creamy top. My recipe does call for a milk frother, but on the plus side, it's only a few dollars to purchase, and you don't need a cocktail shaker when you want to bang these out. You can easily multiply quantities and whisk everything together incredibly quickly to make more for you and your mates.

Place the coffee, vodka, liqueur, sugar syrup, 2 small ice cubes and 75 ml (2¼ fl oz) water in a tall glass. Using a milk frother, froth until combined and comes halfway up the glass (see Note). Top up with ice. Serve with a metal straw, if you like.

MASTIHA SPRITZ (VE)

Time
5 minutes

SERVES 1

60 ml (2 fl oz) sparkling wine
45 ml (1½ fl oz) mastiha (see Note)
20 ml (½ fl oz) fresh lemon juice
10 ml (¼ fl oz) agave
Ice cubes
60 ml (2 fl oz) soda water (club soda)
1 fresh rosemary sprig, for garnishing

Note
Find mastiha at selected bottle shops.

Mastiha is one of my favourite liqueurs. It has a wonderful, vegetal, earthy and savoury flavour, which brings complexity to otherwise simple cocktails. Now, it's not for everyone, but those who like it, love it. Here, I have popped it in an easy spritz that's well balanced with citrus and a touch of sweet agave. As agave and mastic trees are both slow-growing, hot-climate plants, the pairing of them is a wonderful collaboration. Best enjoyed in the heat of summer, the refreshing factor is high with this cocktail.

Pour the sparkling, mastiha, lemon juice and agave into a tall glass. Fill with ice cubes. Using a bar spoon or chopstick, stir until well combined and the glass is frosted. Add more ice cubes, top up with soda water, then give it a little mix. Decorate with rosemary to serve.

HEMINQUINCE DAIQUIRI (VE)

Time
10 minutes

SERVES 1

60 ml (2 fl oz) dark rum
20 ml (½ fl oz) quince syrup
  (see Note)
15 ml (½ fl oz) fresh grapefruit juice
15 ml (½ fl oz) fresh lime juice
4 fresh thyme sprigs
Ice cubes

Note
For the quince syrup, use the liquid from the Poached quince (page 198).

This is my take on the Hemingway daiquiri, using the reduced poaching liquid from my Poached quince (page 198) instead of the classic maraschino liqueur. As legend has it, the original daiquiri didn't include syrup because Ernest Hemingway was diabetic. It's said to have originated in a Havana bar frequented by the man, creating the now-iconic take on the daiquiri. I have used dark rum instead of white, as dark rum is bolder and richer, and has vanilla notes, which complement the quince syrup wonderfully. Taste-wise, this cocktail is tart and on the sour side with juicy body.

Place a coupe glass in the freezer to chill while you make the cocktail.

Place the rum, quince syrup, grapefruit juice, lime juice and 3 thyme sprigs in a cocktail shaker. Fill with ice cubes, then shake hard for 15 seconds, or until the shaker is frosted.

Double strain the daiquiri into the chilled glass. Garnish with the remaining thyme sprig.

UP TO
60 MINUTES

I'VE GOT AN HOUR

THESE RECIPES TAKE UP TO AN HOUR,

with a clear focus on weeknight dinners. The meals don't require too much effort, with most of the time being spent in the oven or on the stove, giving you more time to kick back from the day.

ROASTED OLIVES (VE)

Time
35 minutes

SERVES 3–4

300 g (10½ oz) pitted kalamata olives
4 garlic cloves
1 lemon
4 fresh oregano sprigs
¼ cup (60 ml) olive oil
Warmed bread, to serve

Note
Don't feel like you have to stick to the exact ingredients listed here. Don't have lemon? Use orange. No oregano? Grab some rosemary or thyme. Run out of garlic? Add chopped French shallot or onion.

I eat olives like they're a bowl of popcorn, but something magical happens when they're warmed up. There are a lot of recipes that gently warm olives in a pan, but I think roasting them works just as well – and it's a lot more hands off. Everything goes into a tray in the oven, then you walk away. This recipe is flexible too. There are so many ways you can go with this, which makes it great for when any unexpected guests come over (see Note). Serve up with warm bread.

Preheat oven to 210°C (400°F) fan-forced.

Place the olives on a small baking tray (don't use a large tray, you want the olives to fit nice and snug). Chop each garlic clove into 3–4 smaller pieces and add to the tray. Using a peeler, cut all the peel off the lemon until it's bare. Add the lemon peel to the tray, along with the oregano and oil. Mix so everything is evenly coated with oil. Roast for 30 minutes, mixing everything together every 10 minutes to make sure the oregano and lemon peel don't burn, or until the olives are blistered.

Spoon the olives into a serving bowl and serve with warm bread.

Time
45 minutes

ZUCCHINI FRITTERS (V)

MAKES 12

KOLOKITHOKEFTEDES

3 zucchini (courgette)
1 brown onion
1 lemon
120 g (14¼ oz) fresh flat-leaf (Italian) parsley leaves
120 g (14¼ oz) fresh chives
120 g (14¼ oz) fresh dill
1 tablespoon ground cumin
1 tablespoon cracked black pepper
3 eggs
200–250 g (7–9 oz) self-raising flour
Canola oil, for shallow-frying
Salt, to taste
Flaky sea salt, to serve

YOGHURT DIPPING SAUCE (OPTIONAL)
3 garlic cloves
¼ lemon
400 g (14 oz) Greek-style yoghurt

Note
The trick to getting the fritters into the oil without splattering oil or breaking apart the fritter is to dunk the spatula in the oil, then lift the spatula and pop the disc of fritter mixture on it, then slide it into the pan. When ready to flip, gently lift the fritter with the spatula and flip so the fritter gently falls off, giving a small tap if you need.

Keftedes, which loosely translates to 'fritters', are a really common way for Greeks to cook up an array of summer vegetables. Whether it be tomatoes to make domatokeftedes, or anything you have lying around from the garden (or bottom of the fridge crisper), these are the go-to if you are low on time and need to get rid of a bunch of ingredients. Like a lot of Greek recipes, feel free to add and subtract ingredients. The most important part is having a batter thick enough that it just holds itself together when you pull it away from the side of the bowl. Don't like dill? Go more parsley. Don't have chives but you have spring onion (scallion)? In it goes! There are no rules for keftedes – except struggling to say kolokithokeftedes every time you try.

If making the dipping sauce, mince the garlic and place in a bowl. Squeeze in the juice of the lemon quarter. Mix in the yoghurt until combined. Season with salt and mix through. Place in the fridge until ready to serve.

Using a cheese grater, shred the zucchini, then transfer to a sieve set over a bowl. Season heavily with salt, then massage in. Set aside to drain.

Finely dice the onion, then place in a bowl. Finely grate in the zest of the lemon. Roughly chop the herbs and add to the bowl, along with the cumin, pepper and a few pinches of salt. Mix together. Whisk the eggs in a small bowl, then add to the herb mixture and mix.

Gently push down on the zucchini in the sieve to squeeze as much liquid out as possible. Add to the bowl and mix together until combined.

Add 200 g (7 oz) flour and mix through until incorporated and the mixture begins to pull away from the side of the bowl. It should be able to just hold a fritter shape in your hand, so gradually add the remaining flour until you get the right consistency.

Add oil to a frying pan until a thumb's width deep. Place over medium–high heat. One at a time, scoop and shape four discs of batter and add to the pan (see Note). Cook the fritters for 3 minutes on one side, or until deep golden brown. (You want to see small bubbles and golden colour around the edges.) Once it gets quite dark, flip and do the same on the other side. Remove from pan and set aside on paper towel to drain. Repeat with the remaining batter.

Sprinkle the fritters with flaky sea salt. Cut the lemon into wedges. Serve the fritters warm with the yoghurt dipping sauce, if using, and the lemon wedges to squeeze over just before enjoying.

GLAZED CARROTS (V)

Time
35 minutes

SERVES 3–4
(AS A SIDE)

3 large carrots
Olive oil
50 g (1¾ oz) salted butter
1 tablespoon ground paprika
1 lemon
3 tablespoons honey
20 g (¾ oz) fresh mint leaves
20 g (¾ oz) fresh dill, plus extra for garnishing
¾ cup (200 g) Greek-style yoghurt
Salt, to taste

Note
To help get colour on the carrots, I recommend filling up a small, heavy pan with water and placing it on top of the carrots as they cook. The extra weight will help get an even char.

When I think about recipes that really changed my following, this is the one. Every Christmas I'll post a variation of this carrot recipe, because people go wild for it – and it's easy to see why. With a sticky, sweet and salty glaze and a vibrant herb sauce, it looks great next to any protein, and kind of makes itself the main star. Previously, I have gone with more Asian flavours, but for this book – as the name suggests – I have kept a Greek mindset (apart from the butter, sorry, but carrots just need butter).

Cut the carrots in half lengthways. Heat your biggest frying pan over super–high heat. Add a glug of oil. Add the carrot halves, cut-side down, and char hard (you want to burn them, see Note). Flip and do the same to the other side.

Reduce heat to medium–low, then add the butter and paprika. Braise the carrot halves in the paprika butter, basting them every now and again, for 10 minutes, or until softened.

While the carrot braises, halve the lemon and squeeze the juice of 1 half into a bowl. Add the honey and mix together.

Finely chop the mint and dill, and place in a separate bowl, along with the yoghurt. Squeeze the juice of the remaining lemon half into the herb bowl and season with salt. Place in the fridge until ready to serve.

Add the honey mixture to the pan, roll the carrot halves through the sauce, then cook for a further 5 minutes, or until a fork easily pierces through the thickest part of the carrot with no resistance. You also want the sauce to thicken and become sticky.

To serve, spread the herbed yoghurt over a serving plate and top with the glazed carrot halves. Finish with a drizzle of the sticky sauce from the pan and scatter extra dill over.

LAMB AND PORK MEATBALLS

Time
40 minutes

MAKES 22–26

KEFTEDES

1 brown onion
4 garlic cloves
40 g (1½ oz) kefalograviera cheese (see Notes)
1 bunch fresh mint
1 egg
⅔ cup (80 g) dry (packaged) breadcrumbs
1 tablespoon ground cumin
1 tablespoon salt
500 g (1 lb 2 oz) minced (ground) pork
500 g (1 lb 2 oz) minced (ground) lamb
2 tablespoons olive oil
Extra-virgin olive oil, for drizzling
Cracked black pepper, to taste
200 g (7 oz) tzatziki (see Notes)
1 Lebanese (short) cucumber

Notes

- If you can't find kefalograviera cheese, use parmesan instead.
- If you've got time, make my more traditional Tzatziki (which requires overnight draining) on page 210. Or if you're short on time, use my Quick tzatziki (page 112).

I have a really clear memory of eating keftedes at a random little taverna a mate and I found on the island of Ikaria. We sat outside and were served shallow-fried balls of minced lamb. As soon as I took a bite, the hit of fresh mint and cumin filled my mouth, and we just couldn't stop eating them. Dipped in freshly-hung tzatziki (drained like labneh), to this day it's still one of my most cherished food memories. This recipe is a homage to that dish, made with lots of mint and cumin. I've used a mixture of lamb and pork mince for two reasons: one, I love the combination of these meats, and two, it's just a little bit cheaper to add in pork to bulk it out instead of just using lamb.

Coarsely grate the onion into a bowl, then finely grate in the garlic and cheese. Reserve a couple of mint sprigs (for garnish). Pick and roughly chop the leaves from the remaining mint sprigs. Add to the bowl. Lightly whisk the egg in a small bowl, then add to the onion mixture, along with the breadcrumbs and cumin. Season with salt and pepper. Mix together, then add the pork and lamb. Using clean hands, mix everything together well.

Grab a large plate or tray and roll the mixture into small to medium-sized balls. (You don't want them too big or they won't cook through.) You should end up with 22–26 meatballs in total.

Place a large frying pan with a lid over medium–high heat, then add 1 tablespoon olive oil. Once hot, add half the meatballs and cover with the lid. Cook, flipping halfway, for 7–8 minutes, or until really caramelised. Place on a plate lined with paper towel. Repeat with the remaining 1 tablespoon olive oil and meatballs.

To plate up, dollop the tzatziki onto serving plates. Cut the cucumber into big pieces and scatter them over the tzatziki. Top with the meatballs and leaves from the reserved mint sprigs, then drizzle with extra-virgin olive oil.

FAVA DIP (VE)

Time
1 hour

SERVES 10–12 (AS A STARTER)

Extra-virgin olive oil
2 red onions
1 brown onion
1 lemon
2 tablespoons ground cumin
5 garlic cloves
1 small bunch fresh oregano
500 g (1 lb 2 oz) dried yellow split peas, rinsed and drained
2 fresh bay leaves (optional)
2 tablespoons baby capers
1 small French shallot
Salt, to taste

Note
This dip will keep in an airtight container in the fridge for up to a week, or in the freezer for up to 6 months.

TASTES EVEN BETTER THE NEXT DAY

Greek dips get a lot of love. Tzatziki, melitzanosalata (eggplant/aubergine dip) and even taramasalata have a very committed following (including myself). But fava dip gets lost along the way. It's the one I get most excited to have when I am in Greece, because it really is just so tasty and underrated. The blend of yellow split peas simmered down and hit with lots of lemon juice goes so well as a dip or with so many different proteins. It can be super smooth or a little chunky, and depending on whose taverna you go to, it's always a little different, but always a winner. Plus, it's made using very simple and cheap ingredients, making it great to make when people are coming over as it yields a high amount, with little work and at little cost.

Heat a large saucepan over medium heat, then add a good glug of oil. While the pan heats up, roughly dice the red and brown onions. Add to the hot pan with a pinch of salt. Sweat down for 5 minutes, or until soft and translucent. Finely grate in the zest of the lemon. Add the cumin and mix through. Sizzle for a further 2 minutes, or until fragrant.

Roughly chop the garlic and add to the pan. Sweat down for 1 minute. Pick the leaves from two-thirds of the oregano sprigs and add to the pan, along with the split peas, bay leaves, if using, a pinch of salt and 5 cups (1.25 litres) water. Bring to the boil. Cook for 30–40 minutes, or until the peas break down easily when pressed between two fingers and the liquid is nearly all absorbed. Using a slotted spoon, skim any cloudy muck that comes to the top while simmering. Take off the heat.

Meanwhile, pick the leaves from the remaining oregano sprigs and roughly chop, along with the capers. Finely dice the shallot. Place them all in a bowl with 1 tablespoon oil and mix together.

Remove and discard the bay leaves, if using, from the split pea mixture. Halve the lemon and squeeze in the juice of both halves. Blitz with a hand-held blender until silky smooth. Season with salt, then spoon the dip into a serving bowl and top with the oregano dressing to serve.

FENNEL AND LEEK BAKED BEANS (VE)

GIGANTES PLAKI

Time
55 minutes

SERVES 4 (AS A SHARED PLATE)

Olive oil
1 fennel bulb
1 leek
1 brown onion
2 × 400 g (14 oz) tins butter (lima) beans, drained
4 garlic cloves
1 orange
1 tablespoon dried oregano
400 g (14 oz) tin diced tomatoes
1 fresh or dried bay leaf
Salt, to taste
Crusty bread, to serve

Note
Drizzling olive oil over before baking and grilling the beans helps them char. You want some little burnt flecks over the beans and sauce.

TASTES EVEN BETTER THE NEXT DAY

Baked beans don't rile me up with excitement, but the Greek version, gigantes, certainly does. Traditionally, this dish is made by soaking large Greek lima beans overnight before cooking, but I have tried to hack the classic recipe, so that you can cook it all up in under an hour. I filled it out with fennel and leek, which goes really well with the perfumed nature of orange. If you're not a fennel fan (my partner isn't, but he still loves this version), feel free to add more leek and onion instead. It'll be just as delicious.

Preheat oven to 190°C (375°F) fan-forced.

Heat a heavy-based, ovenproof saucepan over medium heat, then add a glug of oil. While the pan heats up, roughly dice the fennel, leek and onion in that order, adding one by one to the pan with pinches of salt. (The salt helps the vegetables sweat down.) Once all in, continue to cook, stirring every minute, for 5 minutes, or until everything is soft and translucent.

Increase heat to high and add another glug of oil. Add the butter beans, stir through and cook for 1–2 minutes to get some colour on the beans. Mince the garlic and add to the pan. Finely grate in the zest of the orange. Add the oregano and mix through. Cook for 1 minute.

Halve the orange and squeeze both halves into the pan to deglaze, using a wooden spoon to scrape the base of the pan. Once the orange juice has nearly disappeared (it won't take longer than 1–2 minutes), add the tomatoes. Half-fill the empty tin with water, swirl around, then pour into the pan. Stir in the bay leaf and season with salt if it needs it. Bring to a simmer. Drizzle oil all over the top. (Do not stir, see Note.) Transfer to the oven and bake for 30 minutes, or until three-quarters of the liquid has cooked out.

Switch the oven to grill (broiler) on 250°C (500°F). Grill the beans for 5 minutes, or until charred.

Serve hot in bowls with hunks of crusty bread.

SOUTZOUKAKIA SUBS

Time
1 hour

MAKES 4

¼ cup (60 ml) olive oil, plus extra for grilling
1 brown onion
1 cinnamon stick
1 tablespoon ground allspice
1 tablespoon ground cumin
800 g (1 lb 12 oz) tin diced tomatoes
2 fresh or dried bay leaves
½ quantity uncooked Lamb and pork meatballs mixture (page 96; plus see Notes, below)
4 hero/hoagie buns (see Notes)
Salt and cracked black pepper, to taste
¼ cup (60 g) mayonnaise
60 g (2¼ oz) kefalograviera cheese (see Notes)

ZHOUG GREEN SAUCE
1 tablespoon cumin seeds
3 green chillies (see Notes)
3 garlic cloves
2 tablespoons extra-virgin olive oil
1 bunch fresh coriander (cilantro)
½ lemon

Notes

- You only need half the meatball mixture, but make the full amount and freeze the remainder for up to 6 months to use another day.
- Hero/hoagie buns – long rolls used for banh mi – are important; hot dog buns are too flimsy.
- If you can't find kefalograviera cheese, use parmesan instead.
- If you don't like your zhoug spicy, deseed the chillies.
- The rolls will toast quickly so watch closely so they don't burn.
- Leftovers will keep in an airtight container in the fridge for 3 days.

The meatball sub is the holy grail of food between bread. This recipe is a collaboration between my Greek side and my time on *MasterChef*. Soutzoukakia are meatballs cooked in a tomato sauce. They're delicious as is, so if you feel like serving them with pasta or roasted veg, I won't stop you. Here, I've topped them with punchy green sauce, zhoug. It was a big part of one of my top *MasterChef* dishes, where I covered an octopus with it. I've included two ways to make zhoug: with a mortar and pestle – takes longer but tastes better – or in a food processor. The choice is yours.

Heat a large saucepan over medium heat. Add 1 tablespoon olive oil. Roughly dice the onion. Add to the hot pan with a pinch of salt. Sweat down for 4 minutes. Stir in the spices for 1 minute. Add the tomatoes. Half-fill the tin with water, swirl, then pour into the pan. Add the bay. Season with salt and pepper. Cover, bring to a simmer and cook for 30 minutes to reduce slightly.

While the sauce cooks, make the zhoug. Place a dry frying pan over high heat. Toast the cumin seeds for a minute, or until fragrant and darkened in colour.

If using a mortar and pestle, transfer the cumin seeds to a mortar and use the pestle to break them down into a powder. Roughly chop the chillies and garlic, then to the mortar. Add the extra-virgin olive oil and a pinch of salt. Pound until you have a browny-green mixture. Roughly chop the coriander sprigs and add to the mortar. Squeeze in the juice of the lemon half. Pound until you have a smooth-ish but chunky green sauce. (This will take time and elbow grease, but don't worry; it will come together.) Season with salt.

If using a food processor, transfer the cumin seeds to the processor. Roughly chop the chillies and garlic, then add to the processor, along with the extra-virgin olive oil and coriander sprigs. Squeeze in the juice of the lemon half. Season with salt, then process until well combined.

Roll meatball mixture into 12 balls. Heat a large frying pan over high heat. Add remaining 2 tablespoons oil and meatballs. Cook for 2 minutes each side.

Add the meatballs to the tomato sauce and bring to a simmer. Cook, with the lid off, for 15 minutes, or until cooked through. Discard the bay leaves.

Preheat oven grill (broiler) on 250°C (500°F).

Cut the rolls in half lengthways and place, cut-side up, on a baking tray. Drizzle cut sides with extra oil. Grill until toasted (see Notes).

Spread mayo inside the buns. Top with meatballs and some tomato sauce. Dollop zhoug over the top, then grate the cheese over.

GRILLED BULLHORN PEPPERS (V)

Time
1 hour

SERVES 4
(AS A STARTER)

8 red bullhorn (banana) peppers (see Notes)
Extra-virgin olive oil

SPRING ONION AND FETA DRESSING
3 large spring onions (scallions)
2 tablespoons red wine vinegar
¼ cup (60 ml) extra-virgin olive oil
100 g (3½ oz) feta cheese (see Notes)
Salt, to taste

Notes

- To make these vegan, omit the feta.
- Find bullhorn peppers at the supermarket or try greengrocers.
- All ovens are different. Mine isn't overly strong, so the cooking time is based on that. Whereas some of the new ovens get extremely hot, so the cook on the peppers might go faster or slower depending. Either way, don't stress – the objective is to burn the peppers a bit so it's not the end of the world if yours cook quickly.

TASTES EVEN BETTER THE NEXT DAY

When you think of grilled peppers, I don't think Greek cooking comes to mind, but it should. I grew up in a house where grilling peppers was so common. It's done when bullhorn (banana) peppers are in abundance and enjoyed simply with oil, turned into a htipiti (dip) or placed in brine to enjoy at a later date. My version is a more plated style, and I use the grill (broiler) function on the oven. This means if you only have an electric stove or chargrill pan, you can still char the peppers. Once you do it this way, you'll never look back.

Preheat oven grill (broiler) to high (see Notes). Line a baking tray with baking paper.

Place the peppers on the prepared tray. Drizzle with oil and rub into the skin. Place the peppers under the grill and cook for 15 minutes, then flip and cook for a further 10–15 minutes, or until the peppers are mostly blackened all over.

Transfer the peppers to a heatproof bowl and cover the bowl with plastic wrap. Set aside for 10 minutes to steam.

Meanwhile, make the spring onion and feta dressing. Thinly slice the spring onions, keeping the white part separate to the green part. Place the vinegar and white part of the spring onion in a bowl, along with a big pinch of salt. Mix together and set aside to mellow out the harshness of the raw spring onion and to break down – about 5–10 minutes.

Add the oil and green part of the spring onion to the bowl and mix through. Crumble in the feta and gently mix (it's meant to be a chunky dressing).

Gently peel the skin off the peppers, then remove as many seeds as you can. Tear each pepper in half and place on a serving plate. Spoon the dressing over to serve.

PEPPER AND CUCUMBER SALAD (VE)

Time
15 minutes

SERVES 4 (AS A SHARED PLATE)

- 2 tablespoons sesame seeds
- 1 garlic clove
- 1 lemon
- ¼ teaspoon ground coriander
- 2 tablespoons extra-virgin olive oil
- 4 large Grilled bullhorn peppers (opposite)
- 2 Lebanese (short) cucumbers
- 1 small bunch fresh coriander (cilantro)
- 400 g (14 oz) tin chickpeas, rinsed and drained

This is one of the few times you'll see fresh coriander (cilantro) in this book, because this salad is really elevated by it. It's a great, simple way to incorporate a salad into your dinner without it being boring. Grilled peppers give it a sweetness and the sesame adds nuttiness, which pairs well with the super bright and zesty dressing. It's as delicious as it looks.

Place a small, non-stick frying pan over high heat. Add the sesame seeds and cook, moving the pan every so often, until golden and toasted. (You want a deep golden colour.) Take off the heat and cool.

Mince the garlic and place in a large bowl. Finely grate in the zest of the lemon, then halve the lemon and squeeze in the juice of 1 half. Add the ground coriander and oil. Mix together with a spoon to create the dressing.

Slice the peppers into strips. Using a peeler, cut the cucumber into ribbons. Add both to the bowl. Pick the coriander leaves and add to the bowl, along with the chickpeas. Give it a good mix through.

Serve in a bowl, topped with the toasted sesame seeds.

CHICKEN TRAY BAKE

Time
55 minutes

SERVES 4

1 lemon
1 tablespoon dried oregano
1 tablespoon ground paprika
120 ml (3¾ fl oz) olive oil
1 tablespoon salt
1 tablespoon cracked black pepper
6 garlic cloves
2 zucchini (courgette)
1 red capsicum (pepper)
300 g (10½ oz) green beans
2 tomatoes
2 teaspoons ground allspice
2 teaspoons ground cumin
2 teaspoons ground coriander
1 teaspoon ground ginger
1 teaspoon ground cinnamon
1 kg (2 lb 4 oz) boneless chicken thighs (6–8 thighs)
20–25 pitted kalamata olives
2 tablespoons baby capers
Steamed rice, to serve

Notes

- This will keep in an airtight container in the fridge for up to 3 days or 6 months in the freezer.
- How long it will take the chicken to cook will depend on the oven strength, so keep an eye on it. The chicken will need a minimum of 10 minutes to cook through.

TASTES EVEN BETTER THE NEXT DAY

Out of all the recipes in this book, this is the one I cook the most – almost weekly – for my meal prep. On a Monday, I cook and portion it up – it takes an hour of my time. Some goes in the freezer and some goes in the fridge for midweek lunches and dinners (see Notes). The wonderful surprise with this tray bake is the glorious and silky sauce that comes together from the tomato breaking down slowly with a myriad of spices and flavours going on in the tray.

Preheat oven to 200°C (400°F) fan-forced.

Finely grate the zest of the lemon into a bowl. Halve the lemon and squeeze in the juice of 1 half. Add the oregano, paprika, ¼ cup (60 ml) oil, half the salt and half the pepper. Mince 3 garlic cloves and add to the bowl, then mix all together until combined.

Cut the zucchini lengthways down the middle, then into 1 cm (½ in) thick, half-moon pieces. Cut the capsicum lengthways down the middle and remove the seeds. Cut into 2 cm (¾ in) strips, then into small to medium pieces. Top and tail the beans, then cut crossways into halves or thirds, depending on their size. Add all the vegetables to the spice mixture and mix until coated. Transfer everything to a large tray, reserving the bowl.

Cut each tomato into eight wedges, then toss in the reserved bowl to pick up the last of the marinade. Nestle the tomato wedges, skin-side up, between the vegetables on the tray, reserving the bowl. Roast for 15 minutes.

While the vegetables roast, build the chicken marinade in the reserved bowl. Add the allspice, cumin, coriander, ginger, cinnamon and remaining ¼ cup (60 ml) oil, salt and pepper. Mince the remaining 3 garlic cloves and add to the bowl, then mix all together into a smooth marinade. Add the chicken and, using clean hands, massage the marinade into the chicken.

Once the vegetables have roasted for 15 minutes, take the tray out of the oven. Switch the oven to grill (broiler) on 250°C (500°F). Sprinkle the olives and capers over the vegetables, then place the marinated chicken pieces on top. Cook under the grill for 10–12 minutes, or until you have some nice charred colour on the chicken (see Notes). Take the tray out of the oven and finish by squeezing the juice of the remaining lemon half over.

This is best served with rice to soak up all the beautiful juices created in the bottom of the tray.

TURKISH GRAIN SALAD (VE)

Time
35 minutes

SERVES 6 (AS A SIDE)

1 cup (200 g) coarse bulgur (cracked wheat)
1 cup (155 g) pumpkin seeds (pepitas)
½ cup (75 g) sunflower seeds
1 red onion
1 green capsicum (pepper)
1 cup (140 g) currants
400 g (14 oz) tin lentils, rinsed and drained
1 bunch fresh mint
1 bunch fresh flat-leaf (Italian) parsley
1 pomegranate
Salt, to taste

DRESSING
1 garlic clove
½ lemon
1 tablespoon Dijon mustard
¼ cup (60 ml) extra-virgin olive oil
2 tablespoons red wine vinegar

A lot of Greek cooking makes its way through Turkey. As you might know, the Turkish occupied a large part of Greece for many years, and so a lot of Greek cuisine crosses over with Turkish food. My yiayia loved to use coarse bulgur; it's a cracked wheat, quickly simmered in water which, when added to a salad, brings all the punchy flavours together. My grain salad is super nutty from the toasted seeds, with pops of sweetness from the currants, and a vinaigrette to bring it all together. It's a wonderful all-rounder. This recipe is designed to make the salad in 35 minutes, so there is a bit of multi-tasking involved. If you feel more comfortable focusing on one thing at a time, feel free to – it just might take a bit longer.

Bring 1½ cups (375 ml) water and a pinch of salt to the boil in a small saucepan over high heat. While the water heats up, wash the bulgur in a bowl, then drain. Once the water is boiling, add the bulgur and bring back to the boil. Reduce heat to medium–low, cover and cook for 12 minutes, or until you can easily bite into one grain. Take off the heat. Set aside for 10 minutes, then fluff up the grains with a fork.

Place the seeds in a small non-stick frying pan over medium–high heat. Cook, tossing every minute, for 10 minutes, or until evenly toasted.

While the bulgur is cooking and the seeds are toasting, prep the rest of the salad next to the stove so you can keep an eye on the seeds at the same time. Finely chop the onion, cut the capsicum into small cubes, and transfer both to a large salad bowl. Add the currants and lentils. Pick the mint leaves and just tear the top of the parleys stems off so you grab most of the leaves, then roughly chop them all together and add to the salad bowl. Halve the pomegranate, then smack it with the back of a heavy knife on the skin side to make the seeds fall out into a separate bowl. Once all the seeds are smacked out, collect and discard any white pith from the bowl. Add the pomegranate seeds to the salad bowl.

To make the dressing, mince the garlic and place in a jar. Squeeze in the juice of the lemon half. Add the mustard, oil, vinegar and a pinch of salt. Seal and shake until well combined. Season with more salt.

Add the bulgur, toasted seeds and dressing to the salad bowl. Using a large spoon, give everything a mix through and season with salt if it needs it.

PAPOUTSAKIA PARMA

Time
55 minutes

MAKES 4

2 large eggplants (aubergines)
Olive oil
75 g (2½ oz) mozzarella cheese
75 g (2½ oz) kefalograviera cheese (see Notes)
150 g (5½ oz) shaved ham
Salt, to taste
2 fresh basil sprigs

QUICK BASIL RED SAUCE
1 brown onion
4 garlic cloves
3 fresh basil sprigs
400 g (14 oz) tin diced tomatoes
3 fresh bay leaves

Notes

- If you can't find kefalograviera cheese, use parmesan instead.
- Allow the parmas to grill until the cheese is browned and charred. The time this takes will depend on the strength of your grill (broiler) – keep an eye on it so it doesn't burn.

No matter what you call it in Australia (I think parma is the only correct way), this recipe is a hybrid that brings together the Greek dish melitzanes papoutsakia and Aussie pub classic the parma (chicken schnitzel covered in marinara sauce, mozzarella and sometimes ham). Melitzanes papoutsakia are eggplants baked until the flesh breaks down, then topped with beef ragu and bechamel. Papoutsakia means 'little shoes', which is what the filled eggplants look like once cooked. It's crazy delicious, but it takes a fair bit of time. So, try this recipe – it can be done in an hour – to satisfy that parma craving without being too heavy either. The parma is my favourite meal when I head out for dinner, so it makes sense that I'd create my own Greek version.

Preheat oven to 180°C (350°F) fan-forced. Line a baking tray with baking paper.

Cut the eggplants in half lengthways, then use the knife to score a crosshatch pattern into the flesh, cutting close to the skin but not going all the way through. Drizzle with oil. Season the cut side with salt, then place, cut-side down, on the prepared tray. Roast for 30–35 minutes, or until the eggplant flesh is soft enough to press into.

While the eggplant roasts, make the quick basil red sauce. Heat a saucepan over medium heat, then add 1 tablespoon oil. Quickly dice the onion, then add to the pan with a big pinch of salt. Sauté for 5 minutes to soften, adding a little water if needed so it doesn't get any colour. Finely chop the garlic and add to the pan. Mix through and cook for 1 minute. Break the basil sprigs in half and add to the pan, along with the tomatoes, bay leaves and 1 cup (250 ml) water. Mix through, then bring to a gentle simmer. Cook for 25 minutes, or until thick with very little liquid left. Season with salt to taste, then remove the bay leaves.

Grate the mozzarella and kefalograviera, and mix together in a bowl.

Once the eggplant is cooked, take out of the oven. Switch the oven to grill (broiler) on 250°C (500°F). Flip the eggplant over so it's cut-side up. Using a fork, push down on the flesh so it's all mushed. Pour the red sauce evenly over each eggplant half. Top with the ham, then the cheese mixture. Grill for 3–7 minutes, or until melted and charred (see Notes). Take out of the oven.

Pick the leaves from the basil sprigs, then scatter them over the parmas to serve.

GARLIC ZUCCHINI (VE)

Time
45 minutes

SERVES 3–4

3 large zucchini (courgette)
3 garlic cloves
1 tablespoon ground paprika
1 tablespoon garlic powder
2 teaspoons onion powder
140–160 ml (4½–5¼ fl oz) olive oil
Salt and cracked black pepper, to taste
Flaky sea salt, to serve (see Notes)

QUICK GREMOLATA
1 bunch fresh flat-leaf (Italian) parsley
2 spring onions (scallions)
2 garlic cloves
2 tablespoons white wine vinegar
80–100 ml (2½–3½ fl oz) olive oil, plus extra if needed

Notes

- If you don't have flaky sea salt, regular salt is fine.
- It's important to season the zucchini with salt when serving, as a lot of the salt is removed when patting the zucchini dry, and zucchini really needs seasoning!

Zucchini (courgette) and garlic are a marriage that has stood the test of time. If they were a couple, they'd be the reliable duo all their mates could count on. I grew up eating a lot of zucchini – in stews, fried or cooked off in some olive oil. I wanted the taste of zucchini I grew up with, but simpler and less labour-intensive. This is one tray, an easy marinade and a punchy sauce, not to mention the rich and soft zucchini. Scoring the zucchini flesh in a crosshatch pattern and grilling in olive oil gives it a deep caramelisation.

Preheat oven to 240°C (475°F) fan-forced.

Using a sharp knife, top and tail the zucchini, then halve lengthways. Score a diamond pattern into the cut side of each half. Place on a baking tray and season with salt to draw out the liquid. Set aside for 10 minutes.

Meanwhile, mince the garlic and place it in a bowl, along with the paprika, garlic powder, onion powder, ¼ cup (60 ml) olive oil, a pinch of salt and a dash of water to loosen.

Using paper towel, pat dry the zucchini on the salted side to remove excess liquid. Line the baking tray with baking paper. Massage the garlic mixture into the zucchini halves. Place, cut-side down, on the prepared tray and roast for 10 minutes.

Remove the tray from the oven. Switch the oven to fan-forced grill (broiler) on 250°C (500°F). Flip the zucchini and spoon any of the garlic mixture in the tray over the top. Grill for 10 minutes, or until you have a lovely colour and the zucchini flesh is charred.

While the zucchini is grilling, make the quick gremolata. Pick the parsley leaves and finely chop, along with the spring onions. Place both in a bowl. Mince the garlic and add to the bowl, along with the vinegar, 5–6 cracks of pepper and enough oil to make the sauce loose and not too chunky. Season with salt.

Arrange the charred zucchini on a serving platter. Top with the gremolata and a pinch of flaky salt (see Notes).

CABBAGE ROLL SOUP

Time
1 hour

SERVES 5–6

LAHANODOLMADES SOUPA

MEATBALLS
- 1 small brown onion
- 30 g (1 oz) fresh dill
- 500 g (1 lb 2 oz) minced (ground) beef
- ⅓ cup (75 g) arborio rice
- 1 tablespoon ground cinnamon (see Note)
- Salt and cracked black pepper, to taste

SOUP
- 2 tablespoons olive oil
- 1 brown onion
- 3 garlic cloves
- 4 cups (1 litre) chicken stock
- 600 g (1 lb 5 oz) green cabbage
- ⅓ cup (80 g) dried orzo or risoni pasta

Note
The cinnamon is really important in the meatballs as it soaks up the moisture and helps hold the meatballs together. You can swap for plain (all-purpose) flour, if you prefer.

Lahanodolmades are a beloved classic Greek dish of seasoned beef mince wrapped in parboiled cabbage leaves. They are then boiled, resulting in a ridiculously delicious parcels of love. As fantastic as they are, they are also a little time-consuming and really rely on proper technique to get them right. So, this is my unwrapped version in soup form. It has all the flavours of the classic, but it's a lot faster and comes together in an hour. The soupa really latches onto the flavour of the meatballs, while the orzo is a fun addition to help thicken everything.

To make the meatballs, finely dice the onion and dill, and place both in a large bowl. Add the beef, rice, cinnamon, 2 teaspoons salt and a few cracks of pepper. Using clean hands, mix until well combined. Roll the mixture into 15 balls.

To make the soup, place a stockpot or your largest saucepan over medium heat. Add the oil. While the pan heats up, roughly dice the onion. Add to the pot with a big pinch of salt. Sweat down for 3–4 minutes, or until translucent.

While the onion cooks, finely chop the garlic.

Add the garlic to the pot and stir for 1 minute. Increase heat to high, then pour in the stock and 4 cups (1 litre) water. Cover with the lid and bring to a simmer. Gently lower in the meatballs, making sure they're all submerged in the soup. Cover with the lid, reduce heat to medium and simmer for 15 minutes.

While the meatballs cook in the soup, roughly chop the cabbage.

Gradually add the cabbage to the pot and stir into the soup. Add the pasta and season with salt and pepper. Simmer, with the lid off, for 15 minutes, or until the cabbage is soft, but still with a touch of bite.

Serve up nice and hot.

SMASHED PORK GYRO

Time
50 minutes

SERVES 4

800 g (1 lb 12 oz) minced (ground) pork
1 tablespoon dried oregano
1 tablespoon ground paprika
1 tablespoon onion powder
1 tablespoon salt
1 tablespoon cracked black pepper
4 × 20 cm (8 in) flour wraps (see Notes)
Olive oil
Fresh flat-leaf (Italian) parsley leaves and sumac, to serve

PICKLED RED ONION
1 cup (250 ml) apple cider vinegar
3 tablespoons caster (superfine) sugar
1 teaspoon sumac
1 small red onion

QUICK TZATZIKI
1 Lebanese (short) cucumber
15 g (½ oz) fresh dill
2 garlic cloves
250 g (9 oz) Greek-style yoghurt

Notes

- To make these gyros snack sized, swap the large wraps for small ones.
- The pickled red onion and quick tzatziki will keep in the fridge for up to 3 days.

Sometimes, you want to smash a gyro but you don't have the time or patience. Well, this is my smashed pork gyro, which you can cook in under an hour, and it hits that craving so nicely. This is my base recipe for the pork, with a quick tzatziki and pickled red onion. From there, have some fun with the fillings. Fresh-cut tomato and lettuce is my go-to as it adds great crunch and freshness. Or try thinly sliced red cabbage and grated carrot to bulk it out.

To make the pickled red onion, place the vinegar, sugar and sumac in a small saucepan over medium heat and bring to the boil. While the pickling liquid heats up, halve the onion, then thinly slice. Place in a heatproof container. Pour the simmering pickling liquid over the onion. Cover with the lid and set aside to pickle while you make the tzatziki and pork gyro.

To make the quick tzatziki, grate the cucumber into a sieve, add a pinch of salt and massage it in. Set the sieve over the sink to drain. While the cucumber drains, finely chop the dill, mince the garlic and place both in a bowl, along with the yoghurt. Mix it all together, then season with salt to taste. Squeeze as much liquid out of the grated cucumber as possible, then mix into the yoghurt mixture. Place in the fridge until ready to serve.

Place the pork, oregano, paprika, onion powder, salt and pepper in a large bowl. Using clean hands, mix it all together until combined. Divide the pork mixture among the wraps, using your hands to spread the mixture over the wraps and pushing it all the way to the edge (you want it to the edge as the mixture will shrink as it cooks in the pan).

Heat a heavy-based, non-stick frying pan over medium heat, then add a little drizzle of oil. Place a pork wrap, filling-side down, in the pan and press down with a spatula. Sizzle for 5 minutes without touching it. Flip and sear the other side for 30 seconds, then remove from the pan. Cover to keep warm. Repeat to cook the remaining wraps, regreasing the pan with oil between each one.

To serve, add dollops of tzatziki and some pickled red onion to each wrap. Roughly chop the parsley, then sprinkle on top of the wraps. Finish with a little sumac.

PORK CHOPS AND SLAW

Time
50 minutes

SERVES 4

BRIZONA ME LAHANOSALATA

4 (about 1 kg/2 lb 4 oz) bone-in pork chops
4 garlic cloves
½ lemon
1 tablespoon dried oregano
1 tablespoon Dijon mustard
¼ cup (60 ml) extra-virgin olive oil, plus extra for frying
Salt, to taste

SLAW
200 g (7 oz) red cabbage
200 g (7 oz) green cabbage
5 spring onions (scallions)
1 carrot
30 g (1 oz) fresh flat-leaf (Italian) parsley sprigs
½ lemon
1 tablespoon white wine vinegar
1 tablespoon extra-virgin olive oil

Notes

- You can also cook the pork on a barbecue. Follow the same method, but keep an eye on how quickly it cooks. The marinade will keep the pork juicy, so you can cook it for over 4 minutes if necessary.
- The cooking time for the pork depends on thickness, size and heat. It honestly changes every time. I like a solid, even heat. A good rule of thumb is when the colour on the sides turns from raw to more white, it will be completely cooked through.
- Got leftovers? Chop the pork into cubes and add to the slaw for a pork salad lunch the next day.

Juicy pork chops are a staple in Greek kitchens. Paired with a super bright coleslaw, this really is a great weeknight meal. The pork gets to steep in the marinade as the coleslaw comes together, then it's a pretty quick cook. My yiayia used to make this as a staple, but as all Greek kids know, her specialty was overcooking meats. Chops are great because they cook fast. Lahanosalata is another Greek favourite. This is a salad I keep going back to, as there isn't any mayo in it like classic coleslaws. It's so fresh and crunchy without being bitter.

Prepare the pork by making little vertical slits in the fat, spaced about a thumb's width apart. (This helps the pork fat render and lets the marinade get into the meat. Make sure to cut just through the fat but stop at the meat.)

Mince the garlic and place in a bowl. Squeeze in the juice of the lemon half, then add the oregano, mustard, oil and a decent pinch of salt. Mix together until the marinade is homogeneous. Add the pork to the bowl and massage in the marinade.

To make the slaw, thinly slice the red and green cabbages, and add to a large bowl with a decent pinch of salt. Massage the salt into the cabbage and set aside to wilt. While the cabbage wilts, thinly slice the spring onions, and peel and grate the carrot (I like to use a box peeler, which catches the grated carrot, but a regular box grater is also fine). Pick the parsley leaves and roughly chop. Add it all to the cabbage bowl. Squeeze in the juice of the lemon half. Add the vinegar and oil. Give everything a solid toss, then place in the fridge until ready to serve.

Heat a large frying pan over medium–high heat (see Notes), then add a drizzle of extra oil. In batches if necessary, cook the pork for up to 4 minutes on each side, pushing down at the beginning to get some really nice colour, or until the pork has a deep char (even a little burnt is great with this marinade, see Notes). Remove from the pan and rest for at least 5 minutes.

To plate up, divide the slaw among serving plates and serve with the pork to enjoy all together.

BRAISED OCTOPUS

Time
55 minutes

SERVES 4

1 brown onion
3 garlic cloves
1 lemon
4 fresh or dried bay leaves
1 tablespoon black peppercorns
1 kg (2 lb 4 oz) octopus (see Notes)
2 tablespoons olive oil (optional)
Flaky sea salt, to taste
Zhoug green sauce, to serve (page 100)

Notes

- Frozen octopus is great, because the freezing process naturally tenderises it. Just be sure to thaw in the fridge before starting this recipe.
- A cartouche is a piece of baking paper used as a false lid in cooking. It allows everything to cook thoroughly but gently underneath without using a lid, which traps the heat. To create one, grab a square of baking paper and cut into a circle to fit the pan. Cut a couple of little holes in it to allow the heat and air to distribute, and place in the pan so it's floating on top of the tentacles.

Greece is synonymous with octopus, and for good reason. You'll see them on every Greek island, hanging out the front of tavernas, freshly caught that morning. Watching the fishermen swinging the octopus into the rocks to help tenderise them is a core memory that brings me so much joy. This recipe was one of my winning dishes on *MasterChef*, where the judges exclaimed that 'it took them to the Greek Islands'. I don't think there is a higher compliment than that.

Quarter the onion and mince the garlic, and place both in a large saucepan. Using a peeler, cut all the peel off the lemon until it's bare. Add the lemon peel to the pan, along with the bay leaves and peppercorns. Fill with enough water to submerge the octopus when it's added later. Bring the mixture to the boil over high heat.

Cut the octopus between the tentacles to separate. Wrap the tentacles in plastic wrap in one bundle. Using a rolling pin, roll over the bundle with medium pressure to help tenderise the tentacles.

Once the onion mixture is boiling, unwrap the octopus and dip each tentacle in and out of the mixture three times to make the tentacle curl. Lower the curled tentacles into the pan. Cover the surface of the water with a cartouche (see Notes) and simmer for 35–40 minutes, or until the thickest part of the octopus is fork-tender. Using tongs, remove from the pan.

You can enjoy the braised octopus as is, or do what I prefer to do: heat a chargrill pan or barbecue grill plate on high until ripping hot. Roll the octopus in the oil, then grill, turning, for 3–4 minutes, or until the tentacles are charred all over and have some smoky depth of flavour.

Cut the lemon into wedges. Serve up the octopus sprinkled with a big pinch of sea salt and a squeeze of lemon juice, with zhoug on the side.

WILTED WEEDS (VE)

Time
40 minutes

SERVES 2

HORTA

2 tablespoons olive oil
1 red onion
1 lemon
600 g (1 lb 5 oz) English spinach
1 large tomato
40 g (1½ oz) fresh dill
Salt, to taste

One of the main reasons I love heading to Greece is the fact that I get to have a plate of horta with every meal, which is essentially just boiled local weeds. It comes in a bowl, wilted down and covered in lemon juice and olive oil. It really makes me feel like I am getting my health back on track every time I eat it. Common weeds used in horta include amaranth and a variety of dandelions, or sometimes chicory (witlof), but as they're not readily available, I have used regular spinach – stems and all. The cook time is for spinach, but if you are able to source some more hearty weeds, then you may need a little bit more cooking time. My version takes inspiration from a variation with onion, tomato and dill, which I have stumbled across a few times. It gives the dish more body and makes the spinach more interesting.

Heat a large saucepan over medium–low heat, then add 1 tablespoon oil. While the pan heats up, roughly dice the onion and finely grate the zest of the lemon. Add both to the pan, with a pinch of salt. Sweat down for 5 minutes, or until softened and fragrant.

While the onion sweats, trim the roots off the spinach and grate the tomato into a bowl, discarding the skin. Finely chop the dill.

Add the tomato, spinach and dill to the pan. Increase heat to medium. Halve the lemon and squeeze in the juice of 1 half. Add a big pinch of salt, then mix everything together with a wooden spoon, helping wilt the spinach as you do. Once the spinach is nearly wilted, add ½ cup (125 ml) water and bring to a simmer. Cook for 20 minutes. It's ready when the liquid is nearly gone and the spinach is dull green in colour. Take off the heat and keep stirring for 1 more minute so nothing burns. Season with salt.

Transfer the horta to a serving bowl and drizzle with the remaining 1 tablespoon oil. Squeeze the juice of the remaining lemon half over just before serving.

WILTED WEEDS PASTA (V)

Time
40 minutes

SERVES 2

HORTA ORZO

2 tablespoons olive oil
1 red onion
1 lemon
600 g (1 lb 5 oz) English spinach
1 large tomato
40 g (1½ oz) fresh dill
½ cup (120 g) dried orzo or risoni pasta
50 g (1¾ oz) feta cheese
Salt, to taste

Notes

- To make this pasta vegan, omit the feta.
- Once you've added the pasta, make sure to stir every couple of minutes to stop the orzo sticking to the base of the pan.

Horta is delicious, but you can turn it into more of a meal and have it as a weeknight plate, as opposed to a side of vegetables (see Wilted weeds, page 118), just by adding a couple of ingredients. Orzo – the small, delicious, rice-shaped pasta – is thrown in halfway through the cook to create a spinach almost-risotto. It comes together really quickly, is full of flavour and is light and healthy.

Follow the method for the Wilted weeds (page 118). Once you've added the water in the third step, bring to a simmer and cook for 10 minutes, or until reduced.

Add the pasta and mix through. Simmer for a further 10 minutes, or until the pasta is al dente (see Notes). Drizzle with the remaining 1 tablespoon oil, squeeze the juice of the remaining lemon half over the top and mix through.

Serve with the feta crumbled on top and seasoned with salt.

MARIA'S BURNT PEAS (V)

Time
55 minutes

SERVES 2–4

1 brown onion
2 small white potatoes
1 lemon
500 g (1 lb 2 oz) frozen peas, thawed
¼ cup (60 ml) olive oil, plus extra for drizzling
Salt and cracked black pepper, to taste
50 g (1¾ oz) feta cheese

Notes

- To make this dish vegan, omit the feta.
- It's really important that the oven grill (broiler) and fan-forced settings are on at the same time for all the roasting time. If your oven doesn't have this option, you can just use the grill setting.

This is a Yiayia Maria specialty. Now, I don't believe it's traditional, but this dish of burnt peas is on the table at all our family gatherings. The dish it comes closest to is arakas latheros (pea and potato stew), which is done on the stove. It usually has a red sauce and a hit of dill, so this is quite different. It's so easy to put together and the result is a mixture of burnt peas and caramelised potato and onion, rolled through the oily lemon juices and bursting with sweetness. I could eat bowls of it! If you want to bulk it out, double the peas and let it cook for a bit longer to get that generous caramelisation.

Preheat oven fan-forced grill (broiler) to 250°C (500°F, see Notes).

Roughly dice the onion. Peel the potatoes and cut into small cubes just a tad bigger than the peas. Add both to a large baking tray. Finely grate the zest of the lemon over the top, then halve the lemon and squeeze in the juice of 1 half. Add the peas, oil, 1 teaspoon salt and pepper to taste. Using a spoon, mix everything together, then drizzle with a little extra oil. Roast for 10 minutes.

Take the tray out of the oven. Reduce oven to 200°C (400°F), keeping it on both the fan and grill setting. Mix everything on the tray again, then roast for a further 30–35 minutes, or until you have a nice mix of burnt peas and some lovely char on everything. Take out of the oven and immediately squeeze the juice of the remaining lemon half over the top, then season with salt to taste.

Finely grate the feta over everything while it's hot, so it gently softens on top, then serve.

STICKY FIG PUDDING WITH OLIVE OIL BUTTERSCOTCH

Time
1 hour

SERVES 6–8

- 190 g (6¾ oz) dried figs
- 1 teaspoon bicarbonate of soda (baking soda)
- 300 ml (10½ fl oz) boiling water
- 100 g (3½ oz) unsalted butter, at room temperature, plus extra for greasing
- 140 g (5 oz) soft light brown sugar
- 2 eggs, at room temperature
- 1 teaspoon flaky sea salt, plus extra to taste
- 220 g (7¾ oz) self-raising flour, plus extra for dusting

OLIVE OIL BUTTERSCOTCH

- 65 g (2¼ oz) unsalted butter
- 200 g (7 oz) soft light brown sugar
- ¼ cup (60 ml) extra-virgin olive oil
- 100 ml (3½ fl oz) cold thickened (whipping) cream

Note

When making the butterscotch, don't stress if the mixture splits as it comes to the boil. It will come back together when you add the cream.

Living in England brought me a lot of my loves in food, be it the Sunday roast at the pub, the Caribbean food that lined the streets around my neighbourhood, or the takeaway Indian curries I craved every Sunday night. But nothing made my eyes light up more than seeing a sticky date pudding on a pub menu, because it really was the sweetest finish to a meal on a wintry day. This is my Greek take, bringing together the British pub classic with the flavours of Greece in the form of figs and an extra-virgin olive oil butterscotch. You can serve this with ice-cream or just enjoy as is. But be warned: it is hard to stop eating, so maybe invite people over to share the love and prevent you from eating the whole tray yourself.

Preheat oven to 180°C (350°F) fan-forced. Grease a 26 × 18 cm (10½ × 7 in) baking dish with extra butter and dust with extra flour.

Dice the figs into small cubes and place in a bowl. Add the bicarb and boiling water, and mix together. Set aside for 15 minutes.

Cube the butter, then place in a stand mixer with the paddle attachment, along with the sugar. Cream together until smooth and the colour lightens. Beat in the eggs and salt. Add half the fig mixture and half the flour, and mix with a spoon. Repeat with the remaining fig mixture and flour, mixing until smooth and you can't see any flour.

Pour the batter into the prepared dish and bake for 30–35 minutes, or until a skewer inserted into a couple of spots in the pudding comes out clean.

While the pudding bakes, make the olive oil butterscotch. Cube the butter and place in a saucepan. Add the sugar and oil, and bring to the boil over medium heat. Carefully pour in the cream and stir continuously for 3 minutes, or until thickened slightly and homogenous. Season with extra salt, then pour into a heatproof jug.

Pour the olive oil butterscotch all over the top of the pudding in the dish and enjoy nice and hot.

EASTER BISCUITS

Time
1 hour

MAKES 32

KOULOURAKIA

3 eggs
1 lemon
1 orange
70 ml (2¼ fl oz) thickened (whipping) cream
60 g (2¼ oz) butter
½ cup (110 g) caster (superfine) sugar
1 tablespoon vanilla extract
360 g (12¾ oz) self-raising flour, sifted
¼ cup (40 g) sesame seeds

Note
This recipe makes a lot of biscuit dough, so you will find you become better at rolling, and after the first batch comes out of the oven you'll start to figure out what size biscuits work with your oven heat, and how long to bake them for – whether you like them softer or crisper. This can be contentious in Greek culture: do you like a softer biscuit or prefer a harder one that's better for dunking tea or coffee?

When I lived in London, my mate and I thought we would bake some koulourakia for Orthodox Easter, so I messaged Mum to get my yiayia's recipe. The recipe included 12 eggs and an unspecified amount of flour. As we persevered – and with many visits back to the local Sainsbury's – we went through over 2 kg (4 lb 8 oz) of flour and our kitchen became a working bakery for 5 hours as we made enough biscuits for a village. It became clear that my yiayia would bake a batch of koulourakia that would easily last through to the next Easter! I have reduced the recipe to a sixth of my yiayia's, so within the hour you should be done.

Preheat oven to 180°C (350°F) fan-forced. Line two to three baking trays with baking paper.

Separate 2 eggs. Place the 2 egg yolks in a stand mixer with the whisk attachment. Finely grate in the zest of the lemon and orange. Add the cream, butter, sugar and vanilla, and whisk until combined. Whisk the 2 egg whites in a clean, dry bowl until the mixture is white and it holds itself, then add to the yolk mixture. Using a balloon whisk, gently whisk in the egg white. Once combined, gradually add the flour, a little at a time, until a smooth and malleable dough forms.

Grab a small piece of dough (about 30–35 g/1 oz each) and roll into a log. Bring both ends together, then twist to form the biscuit (see Note). Place on a prepared tray (they won't expand much, so you only need a small gap between each one). Repeat until the trays are filled.

Whisk the remaining egg in a bowl. Brush the tops of the biscuits with some egg wash, then finish with a sprinkling of sesame seeds. Bake for 10–12 minutes, or until golden. Set aside on wire racks to cool, while you repeat with the remaining dough, egg wash and sesame seeds to make another batch.

Easter biscuits (page 123).

ANISE POACHED PLUMS

Time
45 minutes

SERVES 4

1 lemon
2 cups (500 ml) white wine
250 g (9 oz) caster (superfine) sugar
5 whole star anise
1 teaspoon aniseeds
4 large, firm black plums
Mascarpone, Chantilly cream (page 71) and/or Cinnamon crumble (page 217), to serve

Notes

- To make this dish vegan, serve with coconut yoghurt instead of mascarpone, Chantilly and crumble.
- You can serve the plums hot straight away (you will have some syrup left over), or prep the plums earlier and pop them in an airtight container, cover with the syrup and store in the fridge for up to a week. They taste even better the next day. Just be sure to cool them completely before placing in the fridge.

TASTES EVEN BETTER THE NEXT DAY

PLEASE, please, please don't be put off by the word anise. Yes, we all have bad memories of Sambuca and horrible licorice hits, but this dessert will change your mind on anise. The anise and white wine poaching liquid handles the plums so well. You're left with such a vibrant, show-stopping red that I truly believe this is the perfect dessert to end a dinner party on.

Using a peeler, cut all the peel off the lemon until it's bare. Add the lemon peel to a saucepan. Halve the lemon and squeeze in the juice of both halves. Add the wine, sugar, star anise and aniseeds. Place over medium heat and bring to a gentle simmer. While the mixture heats up, cut the plums in half and remove the pits.

Add the plum halves to the pan and gently simmer, with the lid on, for 10 minutes, or until a fork pierces the fruit with the slightest touch of resistance. Using a slotted spoon, transfer the plum halves to a serving bowl and cool to room temperature.

Increase heat to medium–high and reduce the poaching liquid, uncovered, for 15 minutes, or until you get a deep red colour and a slightly thick syrup.

Strain the syrup through a sieve into a heatproof airtight container, then gently ladle some syrup over the plum halves (see Notes). Serve with mascarpone, Chantilly cream and/or cinnamon crumble.

FIG, FETA AND WHITE CHOCOLATE CHUNKY COOKIES

Time
1 hour

MAKES 12

120 g (14¼ oz) soft light brown sugar
⅓ cup (75 g) caster (superfine) sugar
280 g (10 oz) plain (all-purpose) flour
75 g (2½ oz) malted milk powder
½ teaspoon baking powder
1 teaspoon salt
100 g (3½ oz) white chocolate
150 g (5½ oz) soft dried figs
100 g (3½ oz) feta cheese
125 g (4½ oz) cold unsalted butter
1 egg

Notes

- Once you've measured out the twelve portions of dough, if you have any left over, just roll into another ball or two.
- Feel free to cook both trays of cookies at the same time, but I prefer to do one tray at a time to avoid dropping the oven temperature too much when adding the trays.

Cookies are a way of life, and when creating a Greek-inspired chunky, moreish cookie, I thought, let's go to the queen of cookies herself: my good friend Emelia Jackson. This cookie base is taken from her chunky Levain-style malted chocolate chip cookies, and really is great for holding my trio of flavours. I beg you, do not be put off by the feta; it offers an incredible tang, which really brings together the figs and white chocolate. White cheeses are used in dessert all the time, and I reckon it's time feta had its moment in the sun in the sweet world. The result is a chunky, melt-in-your-mouth cookie so full of flavour.

Preheat oven to 180°C (350°F) fan-forced. Line two baking trays with baking paper.

Measure out all the dry, room-temperature ingredients, as everything will come together quite fast once you start. Reserve 10 g (⅓ oz) chocolate, then roughly chop the remaining chocolate into shards. Reserve 1 fig and chop the remaining figs into little pieces. Slice the reserved fig into very thin strips (you will push these into the top of the cookies later on). Crumble the feta into a bowl and cut the butter into cubes.

Place the butter in a stand mixer with the paddle attachment, along with the brown and caster sugars. Beat until just combined (you don't want to overwork it). Beat in the egg. Add the flour, milk powder, baking powder and salt, and beat until just combined. Add the chocolate shards, feta and finely chopped fig, and beat until just combined.

Use kitchen scales to divide the mixture into twelve 80 g (2¾ oz) pieces (see Notes). Roll each piece into a ball and place six on each prepared tray. Flatten the dough balls into thick puck-like shapes (as they won't spread much in the oven). Press the fig strips into the tops of the cookies to create a racing stripe pattern. Place one tray in the oven and bake for 14–16 minutes, or until golden brown around the edges (see Notes). Repeat with the remaining tray.

While the cookies bake, chop the reserved chocolate into powdery shards.

Once the cookies are ready, sprinkle with the chocolate, allowing it to gently melt into the hot cookies. Set aside on the trays until cool to the touch, then serve.

HARD LEMONADE (VE)

Time
35 minutes

SERVES 1

1 lemon
½ cup (105 g) demerara sugar
45 ml (1½ fl oz) ouzo (see Notes)
2 fresh mint sprigs
Ice cubes
Soda water (club soda), to serve

Notes

- If ouzo is not for you, vodka and whiskey both work wonderfully as a swap.
- The leftover lemon syrup will keep in an airtight container in the fridge for up to a year. Try it in gin-based cocktails or just mixed with soda water.

Hard lemonade has really had an upswing in Australia, but hospitality kids, like myself, have been drinking it for years. A bit of lemon juice, syrup, soda and your favourite spirit makes the most refreshing drink for summer. I have added ouzo here for a light fennel flavour – please trust me, it really isn't overpowering. But, if ouzo is not your thing (I *will* convert you by the end of the book), you can substitute vodka or whiskey. The whiskey is truly delicious as it's not far from a highball.

Using a peeler, cut all the peel off the lemon until it's bare. Place the lemon peel in a small saucepan, along with the sugar and ½ cup (125 ml) water. Place over medium–high heat and stir until it comes to a simmer. Reduce heat to medium–low and gently simmer for 10 minutes. Take off the heat and transfer to a sterilised heatproof container (for how to sterilise, see Notes page 39). Place in the freezer, uncovered, for 15 minutes to chill.

While the syrup simmers, halve the lemon and squeeze 30 ml (1 fl oz) juice into a glass. Add the ouzo and most of the mint leaves, reserving the tops of the sprigs for garnish. Swirl in the glass, then place in the fridge to chill.

Once the syrup is chilled, remove the lemon peel and add 20 ml (½ fl oz) syrup to the glass. Fill with ice cubes. Using a metal straw or chopstick, stir for about 20 seconds, or until the glass is frosted. Top up with soda water. Give everything a stir to combine, then garnish with the reserved mint sprig tops with the leaves poking out the top of the drink.

Time
45 minutes

GREEK MULLED WINE

SERVES 6

KRASOMELO

10 whole cloves
5 cardamom pods
2 cinnamon sticks
1 orange
2 lemons
3 cups (750 ml) white wine
5 tablespoons honey
3 tablespoons caster (superfine) sugar
150 ml (5 fl oz) Metaxa (Greek brandy, see Notes)

Notes

- Metaxa is an amber distilled spirit from the Aegean islands. It's made using a blend of muscat wines, botanicals and spices. Find at selected bottle shops. If unavailable, use brandy.
- If you prefer a sweeter mulled wine, at the end, adjust with more caster sugar to taste until you're happy.

This is the Greek take on mulled wine. Enjoyed in the winter months, this drink is a combination of wine, spice, citrus and honey. I fell in love with mulled wine while living in London, where every single one of my mates had their own combination. Everyone has something they swear by when it comes to this drink, but I think a simple mix is always appreciated. It's easy to forget that Greece gets cold in the winter months, and a warming, spiced drink to heat up your hands is always welcome! Where my yiayia's side comes from in the north of Peloponnese, when the beach wind hits the town of Aigio, a mug of krasomelo is the only way through it.

Heat a large, dry saucepan over medium heat. Add the cloves, cardamom and cinnamon, and cook, stirring, for 2 minutes, or until super fragrant. Take off the heat. Transfer the mixture to a mortar and use a pestle to gently break down the spices a little bit.

Using a peeler, cut all the peel off the orange and 1 lemon until they're bare, then add the peel to the pan. Halve the orange and squeeze in the juice of both halves. Halve the lemons and squeeze in the juice of all halves. Return the spice mixture to the pan. Add the wine, honey and sugar. Place over medium–low heat and bring to just below a simmer. When you start to see steam, take off the heat and set aside for at least 20 minutes to infuse.

Return the pan to low heat, pour in the Metaxa and bring to just under a simmer. Ladle the mulled wine into glasses to serve (see Notes).

1–2 HOURS

I'VE GOT THE AFTERNOON

THESE DISHES COME IN BETWEEN 1–2 HOURS.

This is where the book really dives into more classic Greek recipes. They take a bit of time in Greece, but these ones have been modified enough that you only need a couple of hours free in the afternoon to achieve them.

FETA AND OLIVE FOCACCIA (V)

Time
1 hour 45 minutes

MAKES 1 LOAF

- 360 ml (12 fl oz) warm water
- 2 teaspoons (7 g sachet) instant yeast (see Note)
- 1 teaspoon caster (superfine) sugar
- 400 g (14 oz) bread flour
- 2 teaspoons salt
- 100 g (3½ oz) feta cheese
- 100 g (3½ oz) pitted kalamata olives
- 1 tablespoon dried oregano
- Olive oil

Note
I recommend using an 'all-in-one' instant yeast and bread improver, or an instant baking yeast or bread machine yeast (depending on where you are in the world). Regular instant yeast works fine too.

No kneading? Tick. Under 2 hours? Tick. Light and fluffy middle? Tick. Golden crunchy exterior? Tick, tick, tick! This is a timeless recipe that I go back to over and over and over again. It just never lets me down. You can really go to town with whatever toppings you like, or even stick to a plain focaccia with sea salt sprinkled over the top. I just find this salty and tangy mix of olives and feta works so well pushed in, and allows the bubbles to form around it. Not to mention the woody and earthy oregano, which hits you in the face with its aroma. It is really hard to stop eating this one.

Place the warm water, yeast and sugar in a large bowl and whisk together with a fork until the yeast has integrated into the water. Add the flour, then the salt and mix with a large plastic spoon (or just a large spoon) to bring it together. Cover with plastic wrap and rest for 20 minutes in a warm spot.

Using a slightly wet hand, slap the dough over and over, and pull the dough from underneath on top of itself to stretch it a bit. Finish by folding the dough over itself on four sides, by pulling one side up and folding over the top, then repeating on the three remaining sides. Cover and rest in the warm spot for a further 30 minutes, or until doubled in size.

Line a small, deep baking tray with baking paper, then drizzle with oil so the base is covered.

Add the rested dough to the prepared tray and fold from all four sides again. Flip over so there's a flat top. Using your fingers, push and spread the dough into the corners of the tray, then rest, covered, for a final 20 minutes in the warm spot.

Preheat oven to 230°C (450°F) fan-forced.

Now, prep the toppings. Crumble the feta into a bowl. Add the olives, oregano and ⅓ cup (80 ml) oil, and mix together.

After the final rest, add an unholy amount of oil on top so you have a layer of oil covering the dough, then spread the feta mixture evenly over the top. Using oiled fingers, press and dimple the dough all over the top, allowing bubbles to pop up and form around the topping.

Bake for 25 minutes, or until a lovely deep colour forms on top. Rest until cool enough to handle, then slice and serve nice and hot.

FRESH PASTA (V)

HILOPITES

Time
1 hour 5 minutes

SERVES 4

250 g (9 oz) 00 flour, plus extra for dusting
50 g (1¾ oz) durum (semolina) wheat
3 egg yolks
2 eggs
Full-cream (whole) milk, to make up the difference of egg weight up to 190 g (6¾ oz)

Notes

- To book fold the pasta dough, fold both short ends into the middle of the pasta sheet so they meet in the middle. Fold the whole sheet in half lengthways.
- You can serve this pasta in my Pasta in verde sauce (page 60) or Chicken and pasta (page 144).

An argument can be made that hilopites is the most famous of the Greek pasta shapes. I find these little pasta squares tedious to make, so I always cut mine into long strips. My yiayia would send over bags of hand-cut hilopites for us, and it was always so exciting because those little squares soaked up so much flavour. The main difference to Italian pasta is the addition of milk into the wet ingredients, giving it a glossy finish and lighter bite. It truly is a favourite among Greeks for a reason.

Mix together the flour and semolina in a bowl, then pour onto a clean, dry benchtop and create a deep well in the middle. Place a bowl on the kitchen scales and tare to zero out the weight of the bowl. Add the egg yolks and whole eggs, making note of the weight, then lightly whisk. Pour in enough milk to make the mixture weigh 190 g (6¾ oz) in total, then pour into the well. Using a fork, slowly draw the flour from the side into the middle and mix in a circular motion. Once the mixture has a wet consistency that resembles pancake batter, grab a dough scraper and fold in the rest of the flour, cutting into the flour over the top with the scraper to combine everything. (The dough should be shaggy.) Dust the benchtop and the dough with some extra flour, then using clean hands, knead the dough for 8–10 minutes. Wrap the dough ball in plastic wrap and rest for 30 minutes.

Cut off one-quarter of the dough in one piece and flatten with your hand. Place a pasta machine on its widest setting and pass the dough through three times to help flatten. Laminate the dough by doing a book fold (see Notes), then roll through the widest setting again. Roll it through the pasta machine five more times, narrowing the settings one notch at a time and dusting the dough with extra flour if getting sticky (to avoid it sticking to the machine). Do another book fold and roll through the six settings again, then do a final book fold and roll through the six settings again. Repeat this process with the remaining dough quarters.

Using a sharp knife, cut the pasta sheets in half and clean up the edges so you have straight lines. Working with 1 sheet at a time, fold the sheet in half and dust with extra flour. Fold one more time, then cut into 1 cm (½ in) wide strips. Toss through some flour.

To enjoy straight away, cook the pasta in a saucepan of boiling salted water for 90 seconds, or until al dente. Drain, then roll through pasta sauce (see Notes).

To save the pasta for another day, arrange flat on trays and place in a cool place for a day to dry out. Flip halfway through (if you remember). Place in a zip-lock bag and store in a dark cool place, such as the pantry.

CYPRIOT HALLOUMI-FILLED PASTA (V)

Time
1 hour 45 minutes

MAKES 24

RAVIOLES

300 g (10½ oz) 00 flour, plus extra for dusting
2 tablespoons extra-virgin olive oil
4 cups (1 litre) chicken stock

FILLING
200 g (7 oz) halloumi
200 g (7 oz) ricotta
2 eggs
30 g (1 oz) fresh mint sprigs, plus extra leaves (optional) to serve
Salt, to taste

Notes

- When grating the halloumi, you want it to be an almost sand texture.
- To book fold the pasta dough, fold both short ends into the middle of the pasta sheet so they meet in the middle. Fold the whole sheet in half lengthways.
- When cutting the ravioles, you can also just cut out rectangles, if you prefer.
- You should end up with about twenty-four ravioles all up, with a little bit of filling left over.

As I was scrolling through ideas for my PASTABOIS series, I came across this beauty. It's as close to a Greek-esque filled pasta as you'll get. From Cyprus, ravioles is a wonderful show of simplicity and the humbling nature of pasta. The dough is egg free and resembles filo (without vinegar, as there's no baking). You don't need many ingredients or a fancy cutter; in the villages, people use a mug or lid to cut out the shapes, and serve them in the cooking broth. Filled pasta can take time to get the hang of, but the #1 rule is to push that air out.

Place the flour, oil and 150 ml (5 fl oz) water in a bowl, then use your hand to begin bringing it together. Keep going until flour is incorporated into a shaggy dough ball. Place on a clean, dry benchtop. Knead for about 10 minutes, stretching the dough as you go. Wrap in plastic wrap and rest for 30 minutes.

Meanwhile, make the filling. Finely grate halloumi into a bowl (see Notes). Add the ricotta and eggs. Pick the mint leaves and finely chop. Add to bowl with a pinch of salt. Mix with clean hands. Place in the fridge until ready to use.

Cut off one-quarter of the dough. Using dusted hands, flatten the dough. Place a pasta machine on its widest setting and pass the dough through to help flatten. Pass the dough through five more times, narrowing the settings one notch at a time. Laminate the dough by doing a book fold (see Notes), then roll through the widest setting again. Roll the sheet through the next six settings (up to the second last setting), dusting the dough with extra flour if it gets sticky (to avoid it sticking to the machine). You should now be able to see your hand through the dough and the sheet should be the width of the pasta machine. Place the sheet on a floured surface and cover with a clean tea (dish) towel or plastic wrap. Repeat this process with the remaining dough quarters.

Down one long side of a pasta sheet, spoon six heaped tablespoonfuls of the filling, leaving equal space between each one. Using a pastry brush, gently brush water on the sheet around the filling, then grab the sheet from one long side and fold it in half so it's covering the filling. Press down in between the filling dollops and push out any air. Press down around the filling to seal. Using a wide, round mug or circle cutter, cut out the ravioles (see Notes). Transfer to a clean, dry benchtop dusted with extra flour while you repeat with the remaining sheets and filling (see Notes).

Place the stock in a medium saucepan over high heat and bring to the boil. In three or four batches, cook the ravioles for 2 minutes, or until al dente. Transfer to serving bowls. Top with ladlefuls of broth for the pasta to swim in. Top with extra mint leaves, if using.

CHICKEN AND PASTA

Time
1 hour 15 minutes

SERVES 4

KOTOPOULO ME HILOPITES

2 chicken marylands (leg quarters)
1 large brown onion
6 garlic cloves
1 tablespoon dried oregano
1 tablespoon dried thyme
1 tablespoon ground allspice
2 teaspoons ground cinnamon
1 cup (250 ml) red wine
700 g (1 lb 9 oz) bottle tomato passata (puréed tomatoes)
2 fresh bay leaves
400 g (14 oz) cooked hilopites pasta (see Note)
Olive oil
Salt, to taste
Grated parmesan powder or regular parmesan, to serve

Note
Make your own Fresh pasta (page 141) or use store-bought dried hilopites and follow packet directions to cook.

TASTES EVEN BETTER THE NEXT DAY

As I was writing this book, I visited the island of Agistri, a 45-minute ferry from Athens. We walked to a little restaurant up on the hill that overlooked the port, and luckily on the specials menu was kotopoulo me makaronia: essentially chicken cooked in a rich red sauce and pasta to soak it all up with. It took me back to growing up at my yiayia's house, where we were served a dish so similar, bursting with woody spices and covered in the worst grated parmesan powder she could find. We had it with hilopites (pasta) that swam in the delicious kokkinisto (red) sauce. The restaurant on Agistri is called Parnassos, and I thank them, because as soon as I ate it, I was reminded why it was so important to have this recipe in the book. It was unassuming and plated terribly, but ultimately so warming and delicious, like many Greek dishes.

Heat a heavy-based frying pan with a lid over high heat, then add enough oil to cover the base with a thin layer. Once smoking, carefully brown the chicken pieces, skin-side down, for about 4 minutes, or until deeply charred on one side. Take out of the pan and transfer to a plate.

While the chicken is browning, finely dice the onion and halve the garlic cloves.

Reduce heat to low, then add the onion to the pan and stir through. Sweat down, without stirring, for 10 minutes, or until soft and translucent, adding a dash of water if it starts to burn. Add the herbs and spices, and mix through. Cook for a further minute.

Increase heat to medium–high, then pour in the wine and cook until the wine is almost all gone. Add the passata. Pour 200 ml (7 fl oz) water into the empty passata bottle, swirl around, then pour into the pan. Add the garlic, bay leaves and browned chicken. Season with salt and bring to a simmer. Reduce heat to medium–low and cook, with the lid on, for 40 minutes, then remove the lid and cook, uncovered, for a further 15 minutes.

Season with salt, spoon onto the cooked pasta and finish with your heart's desire of grated parmesan.

MOUSSAKA JACKET POTATO

Time
1 hour 30 minutes

MAKES 4

4 large russet (Idaho) potatoes, scrubbed
Olive oil
Salt and cracked black pepper, to taste
Fresh chives, for garnishing (optional)

EGGPLANT AND BEEF RAGU
1 eggplant (aubergine)
1 brown onion
1 red onion
5 garlic cloves
550 g (1 lb 4 oz) beef sausages
2 tablespoons dried oregano
2 tablespoons ground paprika
1 tablespoon ground cinnamon
70 g (2½ oz) tomato paste (concentrated purée)
½ cup (125 ml) red wine
400 g (14 oz) tin diced tomatoes
3 fresh or dried bay leaves

OLIVE OIL BECHAMEL
50 ml (1½ fl oz) extra-virgin olive oil
⅓ cup (50 g) plain (all-purpose) flour
2 cups (500 ml) full-cream (whole) milk
1 egg
1 egg yolk
⅛ nutmeg

Note
Any leftover ragu will freeze really well in an airtight container for up to 6 months. It will also keep in the fridge for up to 4 days.

Moussaka is a staple in Greek kitchens, so much so it has infiltrated the mainstream and is loved by modern society. I also love it: the layers, the flavours, the touch of cinnamon and creamy bechamel. It is pretty special. It's also an absolute pain to make. You really are lucky if you're done in 3 hours, and that's before you let it rest to seal and solidify. So, I bring you my own personal creation (if you can't tell, I am very proud of this), the moussaka jacket potato! It takes all the elements we love about a moussaka, but slashes the cooking time in half. The layers of potato turn into a jacket, the eggplant layer morphs into the eggplant and beef ragu, the meat is from sausages, which tenderises a lot faster. Of course, everything has to be topped off with my olive oil bechamel. The ragu is so delicious, I won't blame you if you start making it for pasta.

Preheat oven to 210°C (400°F) fan-forced.

Prick the potatoes all over with a fork. Rub with oil, then wrap individually in foil. Place straight on a rack in the oven and bake for 1 hour, or until a fork easily pierces through with little resistance.

Meanwhile, make the eggplant and beef ragu. Chop the eggplant into small cubes and place in a colander with a sprinkling of salt and massage in. Leave the colander in the sink to allow liquid to drip out. While the eggplant drains, roughly dice the brown and red onions. Mince the garlic. Heat a large saucepan over medium heat, then add a glug of olive oil. Add the onion and a pinch of salt. Sweat down, stirring when needed, for 5 minutes, or until soft and translucent.

While the onion sweats, remove the meat from the sausages and roughly chop into small pieces.

Add another drizzle of olive oil to the pan, along with the garlic, oregano, paprika and cinnamon. Increase heat to high and cook, stirring constantly, for 1 minute. Add a bit more oil, then add the eggplant and sausage meat, and mix through. Sear the eggplant and beef for 2–4 minutes to get some colour. Add the tomato paste and cook, stirring constantly, for 1 minute. Pour in the wine to deglaze, scraping the base of the pan. Cook until the wine has reduced by three-quarters. Add the tinned tomatoes, then fill the empty tin with 1½ cups (375 ml) water, swirl around, then pour into the pan. Add the bay leaves, season with salt and pepper, and bring to the boil. Cook for the remaining potato cooking time (minimum 30 minutes) until reduced and thickened.

To make the olive oil bechamel, pour the extra-virgin olive oil into a deep saucepan over high heat. Whisk in the flour and cook for a minute. Pour in the milk, then whisk hard until the mixture thickens. (It should coat the back of a spoon.) Take off the heat, then whisk in the whole egg and egg yolk super quickly so as not to scramble them. Finely grate in the nutmeg, then season with salt.

Once the potatoes are cooked, take out of the oven. Switch the oven to grill (broiler) on 250°C (500°F). Unwrap the potatoes and set aside until cool enough to handle.

Using a knife, cut a cross on the flat side of each potato, then gently open up by pushing down on the corners of the cross. Place the opened potatoes on a baking tray lined with baking paper. Spoon a generous amount of ragu into the middle crevice. Spoon the bechamel all over the top, covering the potatoes. Place under the grill and char the top of the bechamel. This won't take longer than 5 minutes, but keep an eye on them as ovens differ. (You don't want to burn them.) Take out of the oven.

Finely chop the chives, if using. Plate up the jacket potatoes, sprinkle with the chives and enjoy.

TOMATO BAKED FISH

Time
1 hour 20 minutes

SERVES 4

PSARI PLAKI

5 roma (plum) tomatoes
2 large French shallots
4 garlic cloves
100 g (3½ oz) pitted kalamata olives
20 fresh thyme sprigs or
1 tablespoon dried thyme
1 lemon
1 tablespoon sumac
1 tablespoon ground paprika
1 tablespoon honey
1 kg (2 lb 4 oz) side of salmon,
skin off (see Note)
2 tablespoons balsamic vinegar
Olive oil
Extra-virgin olive oil
Salt and cracked black pepper,
to taste

Note
If a whole side of salmon isn't available, 1 kg (2 lb 4 oz) salmon fillets (skin off) will also work.

If you know a little bit about psari plaki, you'll know what's pictured here looks nothing like it. That's because I have a confession: I don't like how it's traditionally done. White fish is cooked in a rich tomato sauce and I just find it a bit meh. My version is just as easy to do, but it comes together as a marinated piece of salmon topped with a punchy tomato salsa, which offers more texture and depth of flavour. It's also a very hands off recipe and uses the same tray for the salsa and fish, so the washing up is pretty quick as well.

Preheat oven to 220°C (425°F) fan-forced.

Halve the tomatoes lengthways, then peel off the skin. Halve the shallots lengthways.

Place the tomato, shallot, garlic, olives, thyme, a big pinch of salt, a few cracks of black pepper and ¼ cup (60 ml) olive oil in a long, large baking tray. Mix together until everything is properly covered. Make sure the tomato halves are cut-side up. Roast for 40 minutes, or until a deep char (almost burnt) is achieved. Remove the tray from the oven.

Meanwhile, prep the salmon marinade. Finely grate the zest of the lemon into a jar. Halve the lemon and squeeze in the juice of 1 half. Add the sumac, paprika, honey, 1 tablespoon olive oil and 1 teaspoon salt. Seal, then give the jar a really good shake to bring the marinade together.

Reduce oven to 150°C (300°F) fan-forced.

Remove the thyme sprigs (if using fresh sprigs) from the tray and discard. Toss the mixture, then transfer to a chopping board to cool down, leaving behind the tray juices.

To the same tray, add the salmon marinade and mix with the reserved tray juices. Place the salmon on the tray and turn to coat in the marinade. Bake for 20 minutes, or until cooked through. Take out of the oven and rest for at least 5 minutes.

While the salmon is baking, finely chop the tomato mixture until it forms a rich salsa consistency. Transfer to a bowl, add the vinegar and a glug of extra-virgin olive oil. Season with salt, then mix together.

To plate up, carefully transfer the salmon to a serving platter and top with the roasted tomato salsa. Cut the remaining lemon half into wedges to squeeze over right before eating.

CHICKEN EGG LEMON SOUP

Time
1 hour 20 minutes

SERVES 6

KOTA AVGOLEMONO

1 carrot
1 brown onion
2 celery stalks
3 lemons
1 whole chicken (about 2 kg/ 4 lb 8 oz, see Notes)
1 tablespoon black peppercorns
1 tablespoon coriander seeds
400 g (14 oz) long-grain white rice
3 eggs
Extra-virgin olive oil, for drizzling
Salt and cracked black pepper, to taste
1 bunch fresh dill

Notes

- If you have a larger chicken, just be aware it may need some more time to poach. Once torn, the chicken should be blushing pink; that's a good thing as it won't be overcooked. However, if you are a nervous chicken eater, feel free to poach a bit longer so you don't worry.
- As you're adding the stock to the lemon egg mixture, don't worry if your ladle catches a bit of rice. It'll all come together in the end. Also, be sure to ladle in the stock slowly to avoid curdling the egg.
- If you've added the required ladles of stock to the lemon juice mixture before the rice is nearly done, keep the pan on the heat while you wait.

TASTES EVEN BETTER THE NEXT DAY

This is the humble soup that every Greek child knows will fix any sickness or ailment with one warming bowl. Out of all the Greek classics I cook, this is the one I go back to the most. It's super lemony and the tempered eggs give it a creamy texture. You make the stock from the chicken that's shredded into the soup, so it's a labour of love, but absolutely worth it. My recipe hasn't changed much, and it has stood the test of time. My partner will now request it in the depths of winter, so I'll make sure to make a batch and freeze in portions for when the inevitable flu comes around. Feel free to plump it up with leafy greens, like spinach or Tuscan kale (cavolo nero), wilting through at the end, to feed your health more love.

Quarter the carrot and onion lengthways, halve the celery crossways, then place them all in a stockpot or large, deep saucepan. Using a peeler, cut all the peel off the lemons until they're bare. Add the peel to the pot, along with the chicken, peppercorns and coriander seeds. Fill with enough water to submerge the chicken. Cover with the lid. Bring to the boil over high heat. Reduce heat to medium and simmer for 20 minutes. Remove the lid and cook for a further 20 minutes, seasoning with salt as you go (you need a bit so be liberal with it).

Carefully transfer the chicken to a bowl until cool to the touch, then place in the fridge to cool down. (This makes it easier to shred.) Strain the stock mixture through a strainer into a medium saucepan, discarding the solids.

Wash the rice thoroughly, then transfer to the pan with the stock mixture. Place over medium–high heat and bring to the boil, then reduce heat to medium. Gently simmer until the rice feels nearly cooked, but still has a solid bite to it – about 5 minutes off al dente.

Halve the lemons and squeeze all the juice into a small saucepan. Add the eggs and whisk together, then place over low heat next to the rice pan. While whisking, slowly add a ladle of stock at a time to emulsify the egg mixture (see Notes). Keep adding the stock until you've added six to eight ladlefuls.

Pour the lemon egg mixture into the rice pan (see Notes). Cook over low heat for 3–4 minutes, or until the rice has that perfect soft bite.

Take the chicken out of the fridge. Using a couple of forks, quickly shred the meat off the bone and add to the soup. Mix together and gently reheat if necessary.

Finely chop the dill and scatter it over the soup, along with salt, pepper and a drizzle of oil.

PRAWN RISOTTO

Time
1 hour 30 minutes

SERVES 4

YIOUVETSI

20 raw king prawns (shrimp)
1 carrot
2 brown onions
1 fennel bulb, reserving the fronds for garnish
7 garlic cloves
1 tablespoon black peppercorns
1 tablespoon coriander seeds
3 fresh or dried bay leaves
2 heaped tablespoons tomato paste (concentrated purée)
50 ml (1½ fl oz) ouzo
30 g (1 oz) fresh dill
2 celery stalks
1 lemon
1 tablespoon dried oregano
250 g (9 oz) dried risoni or orzo pasta
½ cup (125 ml) white wine
Olive oil
Salt, to taste

HACK THE RECIPE
Use pre-made seafood stock (or just vegetable stock). Pour 4 cups (1 litre) stock into the yiouvetsi pan after deglazing the pan with wine. Use peeled raw prawns too and you'll halve the prep and cooking time pretty solidly.

Note
Searing the pasta when first added to the pan helps stop it sticking to itself later on.

TASTES EVEN BETTER THE NEXT DAY

Greek risotto (yiouvetsi) is a nourishing pasta bake best described as a filling winter warmer. I have traditionally made it with chuck beef or chicken depending on how I feel, but I wanted to take it a step further. I love prawns and the flavour the shells have. It's a little bit ridiculous how easy the prawn shell stock is, considering it's bursting with umami. This recipe is a waste-free number. It might seem like a lot to do, but if you follow the steps, you'll be rewarded with a glistening bowl of goodness.

Peel the prawns, placing the heads, shells and tails in a bowl, and reserving the prawns for later. Heat a large saucepan over high heat, then add a solid glug of oil. Add the heads, shells and tails, and sizzle, stirring now and again, for 5 minutes, or until coloured.

While the shells sizzle, roughly chop the carrot, 1 onion and half the fennel bulb. Halve 5 garlic cloves.

Add the chopped vegetables, peppercorns, coriander seeds, bay leaves and a pinch of salt to the pan. Sauté, stirring now and again, for 6 minutes, or until softened. Add half the tomato paste. Cook for 1 minute, then deglaze the pan with the ouzo, scraping the base of the pan. Pour in 6 cups (1.5 litres) water and bring to a simmer. Cook for 40 minutes, seasoning with salt if needed.

While the prawn stock cooks, use a skewer to poke through the top of each reserved prawn and gently wiggle out the digestive tract and discard. Roughly dice the dill and finely dice the celery and remaining onion and fennel.

Heat a separate large saucepan over medium heat. Add a glug of oil, then the diced celery, onion and fennel, along with a big pinch of salt. Sweat down for 7 minutes. Mince the remaining garlic, finely grate the zest of the lemon, then add both to the pan, along with the oregano. Stir through for a minute. Add the pasta and remaining tomato paste. Stir through for 1–2 minutes, or until pasta is coated and seared (see Note). Increase heat to high. Pour in the wine to deglaze, scraping the base of the pan. Cook until the wine is nearly all gone.

Once the prawn shell stock has finished simmering, set a sieve over the yiouvetsi pan and strain the prawn shell stock into the pan, discarding the solids. Add the dill and stir everything through. Bring to a simmer, then cook for 6 minutes. Add the reserved prawns and cook for a further 4 minutes, or until the prawns are pinkish orange and the pasta is al dente.

Halve the lemon and squeeze the juice of both halves into the pan. Season with salt and garnish with reserved fennel fronds to serve.

STEWED GREEN BEANS AND POTATOES (VE)

Time
1 hour 10 minutes

SERVES 5–6

FASOLAKIA

- 1 brown onion
- 5 white potatoes
- 400 g (14 oz) green beans
- 2 tablespoons ground paprika
- 2 tablespoons dried oregano
- 1 tablespoon cracked black pepper
- 2 tablespoons tomato paste (concentrated purée)
- 400 g (14 oz) tin diced tomatoes
- Olive oil
- Salt, to taste
- Steamed rice or crusty bread, to serve (optional)

For Greeks, fasolakia is a recipe that rests in all the memories of growing up. My yiayia would bring over vats of this red stew every month – oh, the excitement that would envelop me! Not many kids get excited by stewed green beans, but to me, it's what Greek cooking really is. A few cheap ingredients, carefully put together and allowed to simmer in all its glory. I would even consider this a weeknight meal, because of how hands off it is. It's a great way to get vegetables into you too.

Roughly dice the onion. Peel and cut the potatoes into 2 cm (¾ in) cubes.

Heat a heavy-based saucepan over medium heat, then add a glug of oil. Add the onion and sweat down, stirring now and again, for 7 minutes, adding a dash of water if it starts to burn.

While the onion sweats, top and tail the beans.

Add the paprika, oregano, pepper, a big pinch of salt and a glug of oil to the pan. Mix through, allowing the mixture to sizzle for a minute. Add the tomato paste, mix through and cook out for a minute. Add the potato and mix through for a minute to seal them.

Add the tinned tomatoes. Fill the empty tin with water, then pour into the pan. Repeat again so you add 800 ml (28 fl oz) water in total and bring to the boil. Add the beans and mix through. Season with salt, then simmer for 45–50 minutes, checking the seasoning halfway through and adding salt if needed, or until the potato can be easily pierced with a fork.

Serve in a bowl as is, on a bed of rice or with crusty bread.

TASTES EVEN BETTER THE NEXT DAY

VEGETABLE PASTA BAKE ⓥ

Time
2 hours

SERVES 9

BRIAM LASAGNE

2 large potatoes, scrubbed
2 brown onions
750 g (1 lb 10 oz) eggplant (aubergine)
2 carrots
5 garlic cloves
1 cup (250 ml) red wine
700 g (1 lb 9 oz) bottle tomato passata (puréed tomatoes)
1 tablespoon dried oregano
1 tablespoon ground cumin
1 tablespoon ground cinnamon
½ teaspoon chilli flakes (optional)
1 large zucchini (courgette)
½ red onion
125 g (4½ oz) fior di latte cheese
250 g (9 oz) dried lasagne sheets
125 g (4½ oz) Grana Padano cheese
Olive oil
Salt, to taste

BECHAMEL
100 g (3½ oz) butter
100 g (3½ oz) plain (all-purpose) flour
4 cups (1 litre) full-cream (whole) milk
¼ nutmeg

Note
To make this pasta bake vegan, swap the butter for olive oil, use oat milk, swap fior di latte and Grana Padano for vegan cheese and use egg-free lasagne sheets.

TASTES EVEN BETTER THE NEXT DAY

It is still debated, but technically, lasagne has its origins in Greece. I'll let you hit up all the details on Google, but that's enough reason for me to do my vegetable-forward version of the great pasta bake. I deeply love a classic briam (traditionally, summer vegetables baked in tomatoes and olive oil); all things that go well in between layers of pasta. Usually a lasagne will take you all day, but mine is filled to the brim with vegetables and only clocks in at 2 hours of work. Having the briam sandwiched in pasta sheets, bechamel and cheese just makes everything come alive. This is also a great batch meal to make and freeze in portions for a rainy day (it'll keep in the freezer for up to 6 months).

Preheat oven to 180°C (350°F) fan-forced. Line a baking tray with baking paper.

Thinly slice the potatoes and lay over the prepared tray (overlapping a little bit is fine). Roast for 25 minutes to get some colour. Take out of the oven and set aside to cool.

While the potato is roasting, prep the vegetables. Roughly dice the brown onions and chop the eggplant into small cubes. Peel and finely dice the carrots. Mince the garlic.

Heat a large saucepan over medium heat, then add a glug of oil. Add the brown onion and a pinch of salt. Sweat down for 5 minutes, or until soft and translucent. Increase heat to medium–high, then add the eggplant and mix through with some more oil. Cook for 2 minutes to get some colour and char on the eggplant, then add the carrot. Mix and cook for 2 minutes. Add the garlic and cook, stirring constantly, for 1 minute. Pour in the wine to deglaze the pan and cook, scraping the base of the pan, until almost all the wine is gone. Pour in the passata, 350 ml (12 fl oz) water, oregano, cumin, cinnamon and chilli, if using. Stir through, then season with salt. Bring to the boil and simmer for 30 minutes, or until reduced. Once done, season with salt.

To make the bechamel, melt the butter in large saucepan over high heat. As soon as it's melted, stir in the flour and cook for a minute. Pour in the milk, then whisk hard until the bechamel thickens, but not as thick as a typical bechamel (you want it to still have a loose feel). Finely grate in the nutmeg and season with salt, both to taste.

Thinly slice the zucchini, red onion and fior di latte.

Now all the layers are prepped, it's time to put the lasagne together. Drizzle a layer of bechamel, then a layer of ragu into a large baking dish, covering most of the base (doesn't need to be a solid layer).

Next, add a layer of pasta sheets, breaking into pieces to cover the ragu layer. Top with another drizzle of bechamel and a layer of ragu. Add a layer of zucchini, potato, then red onion. Scatter with a third of the fior di latte. Finely grate a layer of Grana Padano over the top. Repeat layering (starting from the pasta sheets) two more times to create three equal layers. Finish off with the remaining pasta sheets, ragu and bechamel on top.

Cover with foil, making sure the foil doesn't touch the bechamel. Bake for 30 minutes, or until the vegetables are soft and a fork can pierce them with ease.

Take the lasagne out of the oven and increase oven to 250°C (500°F) on the grill (broiler) and fan setting. Remove the foil and finely grate a layer of Grana Padano to cover the top completely. Place under the grill and cook for a further 8–10 minutes, or until super bubbly and charred on top, and has some good colour on it.

Allow the lasagne to cool down to seal in all the layers – preferably 30 minutes, but I won't blame you if you can't wait.

NO-FUSS OREGANO ROAST CHICKEN

Time
1 hour 20 minutes

SERVES 4–5

1 whole chicken (1.5–2 kg/ 3 lb 5 oz–4 lb 8 oz)
¼ cup (60 ml) olive oil
2 teaspoons salt
15 cracks of black pepper
1 tablespoon dried oregano
⅓ tablespoon dried thyme
⅓ tablespoon dried rosemary
¼ cup (60 ml) white wine

Notes

- Whether the dish gets dry while the chicken as it roasts will depend on the chicken. A higher quality bird won't seep out as much water, whereas a cheaper one will and you won't need to add more liquid.
- The chicken pan juices make an excellent gravy. Cook out over medium heat with a bit of flour and water until a super silky and fragrant gravy forms.

Dried herbs are a mainstay in every Greek kitchen. My yiayia has been known to bag up mixtures of oregano, thyme, parsley, rosemary, basil and sage in different ratios and pass them over in plastic bags, like the Greek equivalent of an illegal drug syndicate. These herb rubs are used to marinate different proteins. They are such an easy pantry staple to whip out. This recipe comes from a place of not wanting to buy the 'bachelor's handbag' anymore. For those not aware, the 'bachelor's handbag' is a supermarket roast chicken that comes in a plastic carry bag with a handle. They are dry, overcooked and lacking any flavour, so this is the best no-fuss way to make it at home. The combination of a few Greek dried herbs, olive oil and salt might seem simple, but the result always blows me away. It's very hands off and you'll never pick up a rotisserie chicken ever again.

Preheat oven to 220°C (425°F) fan-forced.

Pat dry the chicken with paper towel.

Mix together the oil, salt, pepper, oregano, thyme and rosemary in a bowl to make a herby marinade. Place the chicken, breast-side up, on a baking dish and pour half the marinade over. Massage the marinade in, then turn the chicken over, so it's breast-side down. Pour the remaining marinade over and massage all over until covered. Pour the wine into the dish, then roast for 10 minutes.

Reduce oven to 180°C (350°F) fan-forced and roast for a further 1 hour, or until cooked through and the skin is golden. Make sure to check the chicken as it roasts and if the dish gets dry, add some water (see Notes).

Take out of the oven and baste the chicken with juices from the dish. Rest for at least 10 minutes before jumping in. (This allows the juices to soak back into the chicken.)

OVEN-ROASTED POTATOES (VE)

Time
1 hour 15 minutes

SERVES 5–6 (AS A SIDE)

PATATES STO FOURNO

5 large potatoes
1 lemon
½ cup (125 ml) olive oil
2 tablespoons dried oregano, plus extra for sprinkling
1 tablespoon cracked black pepper
Salt, to taste

A good solid Greek potato recipe never goes out of fashion, and these oven-roasted spuds are a hit every time. It's so simple, doesn't involve any pre-boiling and it's done how the Greeks have always done it: covering them with lemon, oregano and oil, and letting the oven do the work. A delicious accompaniment to any gathering, these potatoes also pair nicely with garlicky tzatziki to dip them into.

Preheat oven to 180°C (350°F) fan-forced.

Peel the potatoes and cut into long soldier shapes. Place in a roasting tray large enough to fit them all. Finely grate the zest of the lemon over the top, then halve the lemon and squeeze in the juice of 1 half. Add the oil, oregano, pepper and just under 1 tablespoon salt. Using clean hands, roll the potato through the mixture until coated.

Squeeze the juice of the remaining lemon half into a small bowl. Add ¼ cup (60 ml) water and quickly mix together with a spoon. Gently pour the mixture into the tray around the potato (so you don't wash off the oil mixture), making sure the mixture is evenly distributed. Finish with a pinch of extra oregano on top, then roast for 45 minutes, or until the potato can be skewered easily.

Switch the oven to grill (broiler) on 250°C (500°F). Add ¼ cup (60 ml) water to the tray around the potato, then grill, giving the potato a toss and shake halfway through, for 10–15 minutes, or until browned evenly. Taste and season with salt.

HTIPITI FILO PARCELS (V)

Time
1 hour 20 minutes

MAKES 20

500 g (1 lb 2 oz) drained roasted red capsicums (peppers)
200 g (7 oz) feta cheese
400 g (14 oz) ricotta cheese
1 egg
2 teaspoons chilli flakes
375 g (13 oz) chilled filo pastry sheets (see Note)
Olive oil
Salt, to taste

Note
I recommend a chilled filo, like Antoniou Fillo Pastry, rather than frozen. If only frozen filo is available, remember to thaw so it's just chilled before you begin the cook.

Htipiti is a fiery dip that brings together sweet charred peppers and salty sour cheese for a wonderful bright orange combination. It's so simple but so tasty, especially when shoved into filo parcels. The key to this is the folding technique, which gives a wonderful crunchy layered top. When we were younger, my mum would grab frozen tiropoitas (feta pies) from the Greek supermarket. They were crimped and crunchy on the top, and when you took a bite, the hot melty cheese would burn your lips and tongue, and the flaky filo would fall from your mouth – it was epic. This recipe aims to do the same, with the fluorescent orange filling bursting with flavour.

Preheat oven to 190°C (375°F) fan-forced.

Place the capsicums, feta, ricotta, egg and chilli in a food processor and blitz until a chunky dip consistency. Season with salt, then place in the fridge to chill while you prepare the pastry.

On the largest clean, dry benchtop surface you have, lay down as many filo sheets as possible. Pinch from the middle of two sides of a sheet into the middle, then repeat from the two remaining sides to make a four petal shape (see pages 164–5 for steps).

Pull one of the petals up and over so it covers the middle and acts as cup to hold the filling. Spoon a heaped spoonful of htipiti filling into the cup. Grab the opposite petal and fold over the top. Fold the remaining two petals over the top so the filling is enclosed. Flip over the parcel and place in a large baking dish.

Repeat with the remaining pastry and filling, arranging them snugly in the dish. (This amount of filling will make about 20 parcels in total.) If you fill the dish before you've used all the pastry and filling, grab another baking dish. Drizzle the parcels with some oil so they're mostly coated. Roast for 50 minutes, or until deeply golden and you have a wonderful crunchy top.

Htipiti filo parcels (page 163).

3
4
7
8

Time
1 hour 40 minutes

MEAT PIE

SERVES 6–8

KREATOPITA

- 1 brown onion
- 3 garlic cloves
- 1 kg (2 lb 4 oz) minced (ground) beef
- 2 teaspoons ground allspice
- 2 teaspoons ground cinnamon
- 2 teaspoons ground paprika
- 70 g (2½ oz) tomato paste (concentrated purée)
- 350 g (12 oz) chilled filo pastry sheets (see Note)
- 2 tablespoons sesame seeds
- Olive oil (you will need a decent amount)
- Salt and cracked black pepper, to taste
- 1 cup (260 g) Greek-style yoghurt

Note

I recommend a chilled filo, like Antoniou Fillo Pastry, rather than frozen. If only frozen filo is available, remember to thaw so it's just chilled before you begin the cook.

The best way to describe this is like a Greek sausage roll. Iconic to Greeks, I couldn't write a Greek book without featuring at least one filo snail. This filo pie is not as well known as others, but it should be. Layers of pastry wrap up spiced mince like a delicious parcel. There are so many ways to make kreatopita, and it changes all over Greece. The yoghurt is the final touch; it cuts through the pastry and meat, and highlights everything beautifully.

Preheat oven to 200°C (400°F) fan-forced.

Heat a large saucepan over medium heat, then add 1 tablespoon oil. While the pan heats up, roughly dice the onion. Add the onion and a big pinch of salt to the hot pan. Stir through and sweat down for 5 minutes.

While the onion sweats, finely chop the garlic.

Add the garlic to the pan and sweat down for a minute. Increase heat to high and add the beef. Cook, stirring to break up any lumps, until evenly browned. Add the spices and season with salt and pepper. Mix through, then cook for about 5 minutes, or until the liquid from the beef reduces by half. Stir in the tomato paste, then cook for 5 minutes, or until barely any liquid left. Transfer the mixture to a heatproof bowl and season with salt.

To set up for the filo wrapping, fill a small bowl with oil and pop a pastry brush in it. Brush a little oil over the base of a circular or oval baking dish.

Place 1 filo sheet in landscape in front of you on a clean, dry benchtop. Using the brush, drizzle a little oil over the sheet, allowing it to spread. Place a second filo sheet on top and press down to seal together. About two thumbs' width from the bottom of the sheet, add a line of beef filling. Scatter some more filling above the line to cover, leaving a thumb's width border free of filling (to help enclose the log). Brush a line of oil at the top of the sheet (to help seal). Starting from the bottom of the sheet, fold the edge of the filo over the line of filling, then roll up all the way to the top until you have a long, sealed log. Tightly swirl the log into a spiral, being careful not to break the filo. Place in the middle of the prepared dish. Repeat with the remaining filo and filling, wrapping each log around the spiral on the dish.

Drizzle the pie with oil, then brush it all over the top. (This is important to get a golden crunch.) Scatter with the sesame seeds, then bake for 50 minutes, or until golden and crunchy. Take out of the oven and give it a moment to cool.

Serve with the yoghurt to spoon onto each wedge of pie.

Time
1 hour 10 minutes

ALL THE VEG FAKES (VE)

SERVES 5–6

GREEK LENTIL SOUP

500 g (1 lb 2 oz) dried brown lentils (see Notes)
1 brown onion
5 garlic cloves
2 tablespoons dried oregano
1 tablespoon dried thyme
1 tablespoon dried parsley
1 tablespoon cracked black pepper
3 dried bay leaves
200 g (7 oz) green beans
1 large carrot
1 large zucchini (courgette)
400 g (14 oz) tin diced tomatoes
¼ cup (60 ml) olive oil
¼ cup (60 ml) red wine vinegar, plus extra 1 tablespoon
2 tablespoons white vinegar, plus extra 1 tablespoon
1 tablespoon white wine vinegar, plus extra 1 tablespoon
280 g (10 oz) baby spinach
Salt, to taste
Crusty bread, to serve

Notes

- Green lentils also work well for fakes.
- When it comes to the vegetables getting thrown in, use whatever you have; just monitor the cook times. Okra is great in this, as the vinegars help break down and remove that slimy texture it sometimes has. Celery, Tuscan kale (cavolo nero), small-cut potatoes, frozen peas or anything else you have lying at the bottom of your fridge crisper. A fridge clean-up really makes this recipe sing – the lentils are a wonderful base that you can add as much veg to as you like.

When you think humbling, village-style, peasant food, fakes is the Greeks' favourite. It's essentially a lentil soup we enjoy during winter. It's incredibly hearty, and it just brings the eater so much love and warmth. The main reason I am fascinated by fakes is how it uses vinegar as a flavour agent in such a wonderful way. Don't be put off by my many vinegars; they all play a different part, and the key is to slowly simmering it all, so it doesn't cook off the acid. I have amped up the classic by throwing in myriad vegetables. They fill it out for a more modern dinner.

Rinse the lentils, then drain and transfer to a large saucepan. Fill with enough water to submerge. Bring to the boil over high heat, then drain.

While the lentils come to the boil, finely dice the onion and roughly dice the garlic.

Return the lentils to the pan. Add the onion, garlic, oregano, thyme, parsley, pepper, bay leaves and 1 tablespoon salt. Top up with water so the water level sits a thumb's width above the mixture – around 6 cups (1.5 litres). Bring to the boil over high heat.

While the mixture comes to the boil, top and tail the beans, then cut into thirds. Peel the carrot and cut lengthways into quarters, then into small cubes. Cut the zucchini the same way.

Once the mixture is boiling, add the tomatoes to the pan. Pour 200 ml (7 fl oz) water into the empty tin, swirl around, then pour into the pan. Add the oil, vinegars and another 1 tablespoon salt. Bring to the boil. Reduce heat to medium–low, then add the beans, carrot and zucchini, and stir through. Simmer, covered, for 35 minutes so it gently bubbles away under the lid.

Stir in the spinach, then allow it to bubble away with the lid on for a further 5 minutes. Take off the heat. Combine the extra vinegars in a small bowl, then add to the pan and stir through. Taste, adjusting with salt if it needs it.

Serve the soup with crusty bread.

TASTES EVEN BETTER THE NEXT DAY

Time
1 hour 30 minutes

PITA BREAD (V)

MAKES 6

2 teaspoons (7 g sachet) instant yeast (see Notes)
Pinch of caster (superfine) sugar
⅔ cup (160 ml) full-cream (whole) milk
⅓ cup (80 ml) warm water
320 g (11¼ oz) plain (all-purpose) flour, plus extra for kneading
2 tablespoons olive oil
Oil spray
Salt, to taste

Notes

- To make these pita bread vegan, swap the milk for warm water.
- I recommend using an 'all-in-one' instant yeast and bread improver, or an instant baking yeast or bread machine yeast (depending on where you are in the world). Regular instant yeast works fine too.

Fresh pita bread is a staple around the world and every different culture has their own version. It's beloved because it's the simplest form of cooking. Not only is it delicious, but it goes with many recipes in this book – from the dips and salads to wrapping up my Oregano lamb shoulder (page 193). It's the perfect accompaniment, especially if you have no bread in the house and want something ready within a couple of hours.

Place the yeast, sugar, milk and warm water in a bowl and whisk together with a fork until the yeast has integrated into the liquid. Sit for 5 minutes to activate the yeast (it'll begin to bubble at the top).

While the yeast activates, place the flour and a big pinch of salt in a separate bowl and mix together with clean hands. Make a well in the middle.

Stir the olive oil into the yeast mixture, then pour into the well. Using your hands, bring together into a shaggy, wettish dough until all the flour has been incorporated. Dust a clean, dry benchtop with extra flour, then knead the dough for 6–8 minutes, dusting with extra flour as you go, or until smooth.

Lightly spray a clean bowl with oil, then add the dough. Cover with a tea (dish) towel. Rest in a warm spot for 45 minutes.

Separate the dough into six equal pieces. Heat a large heavy-based frying pan over low heat. While the pan heats up, use a rolling pin to roll each dough ball on a dusted benchtop into a large, flat circle about 1 cm (½ in) thick, rotating as you roll.

When ready to cook the first pita, spray the hot pan with oil and increase heat to high. Add a dough circle and cook until it bubbles all over and the underside has a golden brown char. Flip and cook until you have little, deeply charred dots on the other side. Transfer to a plate and cover with a tea towel. Repeat with the remaining dough circles, respraying the oil after each one.

CUSTARD FILO PARCELS

Time
1 hour 50 minutes

MAKES 9

BOUGATSA

4 cups (1 litre) full-cream (whole) milk
1 cup (220 g) caster (superfine) sugar
1 cup (180 g) durum (semolina) wheat (see Notes)
2 tablespoons vanilla extract
280 g (10 oz) chilled unsalted butter
2 eggs
375 g (13 oz) chilled filo pastry sheets (see Notes)
Icing (confectioners') sugar and ground cinnamon, for dusting

Notes

- You will need a super fine semolina. I use durum (semolina) wheat because it just melts into the custard, as opposed to the coarse variety, which will make the custard gritty.
- I recommend a chilled filo, like Antoniou Fillo Pastry, rather than frozen. If only frozen filo is available, remember to thaw so it's just chilled before you begin the cook.
- When filling the filo squares, if the custard is too liquidy, either it wasn't reduced enough or it needs a bit longer to chill. You can always place it back on the stove and keep whisking until it gets thicker and some of the water is removed. You will need to chill in the freezer again (the custard can't be hot going onto the pastry).

You never forget your first bougatsa. For me, it was an incredibly hot day in the city of Thessaloniki, when I walked up this hill that just went on forever until I got to my personal Mecca, Bougatsa To Neon. It was a tiny spot serving up what I had been told was the best bougatsa in the region, and it was everything and more. I had never had bougatsa; not growing up or when I went to Greece to visit the Peloponnese, where my family is from – it never made it to my mouth. Honestly, that was for the best, because when I ate this parcel of greatness in Thessaloniki, I became obsessed with the hot custard in flaky filo, cut into pieces and covered in icing sugar and cinnamon. My recipe is in homage to this style of bougatsa. And while it will never be as good as what those artisans achieve, it's pretty bloody good for something you can make in your kitchen.

Place the milk, caster sugar, semolina and vanilla in large non-stick saucepan over high heat. Using a balloon whisk, mix everything together, and when it begins to bubble, reduce heat to medium to keep it steaming with the occasional bubble (so it doesn't burn). Continue to cook for about 15 minutes, or until really thick, making sure you whisk it most of the time, particularly at the end, to make sure nothing burns to the base of the pan. Once you can lift and draw a figure of eight with the mixture and it stays for more than a second, take off the heat.

Cube the butter, then whisk 100 g (3½ oz) into the milk mixture. As soon as the butter melts, add the eggs and whisk in really quickly (so they don't curdle). Pour the custard into a heatproof bowl and place a layer of plastic wrap over the top, making sure the plastic touches the custard surface to prevent a skin forming. Place in the freezer for 30 minutes so it chills faster.

While the custard chills, prep the filo parcels. Place the remaining butter in a small microwave-safe bowl and microwave until melted. On the largest clean, dry benchtop surface you have, lay down as many filo sheets as possible in portrait in front of you. Dunk a pastry brush in the butter, then shake it over the pastry to splatter with butter. Carefully fold each pastry sheet over itself so you have smaller rectangles, then push down to spread the butter. Repeat this process until you have eighteen rectangles in total. (This will make nine parcels.) Splatter with butter.

Preheat oven to 200°C (400°F) fan-forced.

Remove the custard from the freezer and peel off the plastic wrap. Spoon the custard evenly into the middle of nine filo rectangles. (Don't stress if it's not super firm; as long as it holds its shape for the most part, it'll be fine; see Notes.)

To fold up the parcels, fold one corner over the filling to the middle, then fold the opposite corner over the top. Repeat with the remaining corners so you have a squarish parcel. Very carefully, roll it over so the folded side is face down and place in the middle of an unfilled filo rectangle. Repeat the process of bringing all the corners in so you have a double wrapped pastry. Flip over and place on a baking tray. Repeat with the remaining filled and unfilled filo rectangles to make nine parcels in total, arranging on the tray in a three-by-three formation with sides touching.

Brush the tops of the parcels with half the remaining butter, then bake for 30 minutes. Take the tray out of the oven and brush with the remaining butter (microwave briefly to melt again if it's solidified). Bake for a further 10 minutes, or until golden. Take out of the oven and give them a moment to cool.

Cut each parcel into nine little squares, then dust with icing sugar and cinnamon, and enjoy them nice and hot.

1

2

3

4

5

6

NUT-FREE BAKLAVA

Time
1 hour 40 minutes

1 TRAY

300 g (10½ oz) pumpkin seeds (pepitas)
150 g (5½ oz) sunflower seeds
150 g (5½ oz) sesame seeds
1 tablespoon caster (superfine) sugar
1 tablespoon ground cinnamon
200 g (7 oz) unsalted butter
375 g (13 oz) chilled filo pastry sheets (see Notes)

SYRUP
400 g (14 oz) caster (superfine) sugar
1 cinnamon stick
3 star anise
5 cloves
½ lemon

Notes

- I recommend a chilled filo, like Antoniou Fillo Pastry, rather than frozen. If only frozen filo is available, remember to thaw so it's just chilled before you begin the cook.
- When you've layered all the seed mixture and pastry into the tray, if it's filling the tray perfectly, don't worry about creating a border.

My father's Irish side provided a couple of genetic gifts. One being gay, and the other being allergic to nuts. It hasn't hindered me too much in the savoury world; as luck would have it, most Greek recipes don't really add nuts. But in the world of desserts, it is trickier. Until this book, there was one recipe I have always watched people rave about and not been able to enjoy myself: baklava. So, I have made a nut-free version, which is just as good that even someone without allergies would want to eat it. The seed combination gives it a nutty taste (which I know I shouldn't like, but for some reason I crave it). Once the syrup hits, you wouldn't even notice the difference. Obviously, this is what everyone tells me. I'm trusting my family and friends when they say it's very close to the nut classic. Either way, I love it, so you can definitely take my word for that.

To make the syrup, place the sugar, spices and 2 cups (500 ml) water in a small saucepan. Bring to the boil over medium–low heat, then take off the heat. Squeeze in the juice of the lemon half and mix through. Pour into a heatproof bowl and place in the fridge to chill while you make the baklava.

Preheat oven to 180°C (350°F) fan-forced.

Place the seeds, sugar and ground cinnamon in a food processor and pulse until a fine crumb forms (almost sandy in texture, but not a powder).

Grab a deep baking tray that roughly fits the size of the filo. Chop the butter, then microwave in a small microwave-safe bowl until melted. Using a pastry brush, cover the base of the tray with melted butter, then lay a filo sheet in the tray. Brush the filo with butter. Repeat layering the filo and butter until you have a stack of five sheets. Brush with butter, then sprinkle with one-fifth of the seed mixture. (You should still be able to see parts of the filo. This will help connect the pastry together at the end.) Top with two filo sheets, brushing each sheet with butter as you go. Repeat layering with the remaining filling and more filo sheets (always laying two filo sheets between each filling layer and brushing with butter). To finish, lay five filo sheets, brushing each with butter, on top and crumple in any overhanging pastry to create a little border (see Notes). Brush the top with butter, then using a sharp knife, cut a diamond configuration on top, being careful just to cut through the top filo layers.

Bake for 50 minutes, or until a deep golden colour. Take out of the oven, then immediately pour the cold syrup all over. Sit for 5–10 minutes to allow the syrup to get soaked up.

Using a serrated knife, cut into pieces along the diamond pattern to serve.

LEMON AND BASIL OLIVE OIL CAKE

Time
1 hour 40 minutes

SERVES 12

Butter, for greasing
4 eggs
200 g (7 oz) caster (superfine) sugar
1 cup (250 ml) extra-virgin olive oil
½ cup (125 ml) full-cream (whole) milk
1 tablespoon vanilla extract
270 g (9 ½ oz) self-raising flour, plus extra for dusting
Salt, to taste

SYRUP
1 lemon
200 g (7 oz) caster (superfine) sugar
1 large bunch fresh basil

Note
If you can leave the cake to soak up the syrup for longer than 10 minutes, it'll be better structurally, but 10 minutes is usually enough time.

This is a rendition of a very special dish that I created on *MasterChef* for a challenge. Let me peel back the curtain. We weren't told what the next challenge was going to be, but I thought of a dish on the spot and rocked it. As we were leaving the set the night before, the garden looked suspiciously nicer than normal – almost like it'd had a facelift – all while we'd shot the episode. We clicked that maybe the next day's Mystery Box Challenge would have something to do with the garden. So, that night I worked on an olive oil cake that would use all the staple ingredients in the Mystery Box and flavoured it with lemon myrtle. The flavour was incredible. The next day it turned out we were right and my cake, served with fig leaf ice-cream, ended up as the top dish. Lemon myrtle is a little bit hard to source, so this version uses the wonderful combination of lemon and basil. The basil offers a very light, herbaceous note, while the lemon makes the whole cake so addictive. Feel free to top it with extra accoutrements, but I like to keep my syrup cake simple, just as the Greek bakeries do. It's so moist and fluffy, in my opinion it doesn't need anything else.

Preheat oven to 180°C (350°F) fan-forced.

To make the syrup, use a peeler to cut all the peel off the lemon until it's bare, then add the lemon peel to a saucepan, along with the sugar and 200 ml (7 fl oz) water. Place over medium heat. Break the basil sprigs in half to fit them in the pan. (Don't pick the leaves off; it'll make it easier to remove at the end.) Bring to the boil, then cook for 1 minute. Take off the heat, then halve the lemon and squeeze in the juice of both halves. Stir through, then set aside to cool and infuse.

Line the base of a 22 cm (8½ in) round cake pan, grease the side with butter, then dust with extra flour.

Place the eggs and sugar in a stand mixer with the whisk attachment and beat on high for at least 5 minutes, or until light and fluffy. Reduce speed to medium–low and gradually add the oil, milk, vanilla and a pinch of salt. Reduce speed to its lowest setting and, in three batches, add the flour, whisking until just combined. Remove the bowl from the mixer. Using a spatula, fold the mixture to make sure everything is well combined.

Pour the batter into the prepared pan and bake for 50–60 minutes. (This will depend on the strength of your oven, but poke a toothpick into the middle of the cake and if it comes out dry and clean, the cake is ready.)

While the cake is baking, remove the basil from the syrup and discard. (Leaving it in can make the syrup taste off.) Leave the lemon peel in.

When the cake is nearly done, place the syrup back over super low heat to warm up. You want the syrup quite loose, so if it's become a bit too thick to drip down toothpick-sized holes in the cake, thin the syrup with a dash of water.

Remove the cake from the oven, then while still in the pan, use a toothpick or skewer to poke lots of holes into the cake. Spoon the warm syrup over, then let it sit for at least 10 minutes to allow the syrup to soak into the cake (see Note). Remove from the pan and serve.

DOUGHNUTS WITH HONEY

Time
1 hour 40 minutes

MAKES 40–50

LOUKOUMADES

3 × 7 g sachets instant yeast (see Notes)
2 tablespoons caster (superfine) sugar, plus extra 100 g (3½ oz) for dusting the doughnuts
¼ cup (60 ml) olive oil
2 cups (500 ml) warm water
1 teaspoon salt
4⅓ cups (500 g) plain (all-purpose) flour
8 cups (2 litres) canola oil
100 g (3½ oz) Greek honey (see Notes)
3 teaspoons ground cinnamon

Notes

- I recommend using an 'all-in-one' instant yeast and bread improver, or an instant baking yeast or bread machine yeast (depending on where you are in the world). Regular instant yeast works fine too.
- Find Greek honey at specialty Mediterranean grocers or use your favourite local honey.
- If you don't have a cook's thermometer to test when the oil is ready, put the handle end of a wooden spoon in the oil. If tiny bubbles gather around the handle, the oil is ready.
- There are a lot of different ways to pipe and cook loukoumades, but for beginners I find this method the easiest. The dough will be super sticky and stretchy, which is what we want, but it does make it a little hard to handle. Adding oil to your hands helps.

Fried dough balls rolled in honey just sound good, don't they? Loukoumades are a staple in the Greek dessert world. Vendors sell them on the streets all over the country. They are snack-sized and not too sweet, so you can smash a few. This recipe comes from my yiayia's side, where the dough is simple and bubbly. Of course, if you are not used to the dough, it can be a little hard to manage, but do not worry, you will get the hang of it. One of my core memories was meeting different cousins and family members in Athens, and after we had all eaten, we sat down for a massive tray of loukoumades doused in Greek honey from my family's place on the island of Andros. There was nothing like it and that's why I recommend using Greek honey. The addition of cinnamon brings together all the things I love about doughnuts into one. Feel free to go without and keep it classic with just honey, if you prefer.

Place the yeast, sugar, olive oil and warm water in a large bowl and mix well. Stand for 5 minutes, then add the salt and flour. Mix by hand until light and fluffy. Cover with plastic wrap, then sit for 1 hour, or until tripled in size.

Pour the canola oil into a medium saucepan over medium–high heat and bring to 160°C (325°F) on a cook's thermometer (see Notes).

Once the oil reaches temperature, place one-third of the dough in a large zip-lock bag. Cut a solid, medium slit in one bottom corner of the bag. (This is where you will pipe the dough through, see Notes.) You're going to cook the loukoumades in three batches. Grab a knife and dunk the blade in the oil. (This makes it easier to cut the dough.) Push down on the bag to pipe some of the dough out, then using the oiled knife, cut the dough into pieces about the size of a golf ball straight into the oil until there is a layer of dough balls in the pan. Sizzle for 4–5 minutes, pushing down on the balls with tongs to help get an even colour, or until light golden. (You don't want them too dark, so the middle stays fluffy.) Line a bowl with paper towel, then transfer the loukoumades to the prepared bowl.

Repeat with the remaining dough, refilling the bag with the next two portions of dough one at a time.

Meanwhile, place the honey in a large bowl. Place the cinnamon and extra sugar in a small bowl and mix together.

In three batches, roll the loukoumades through the honey, allowing the excess to drip back into the bowl. Place them on a serving plate and dust with the cinnamon sugar until well covered, then dive in.

EASTER BISCUIT ICE-CREAM SANDWICH

Time
1 hour 15 minutes

MAKES 6–8

KOULOURAKIA ICE-CREAM SANDWICH

OLIVE OIL ICE-CREAM
2 cups (500 ml) thickened (whipping) cream
1 cup (250 ml) full-cream (whole) milk
140 g (5 oz) caster (superfine) sugar
2 eggs
⅔ cup (160 ml) extra-virgin olive oil
Salt, to taste

LEMON KOULOURAKIA
2 eggs
30 g (1 oz) butter
35 ml (1 fl oz) thickened (whipping) cream
¼ cup (55 g) caster (superfine) sugar
½ teaspoon lemon zest
180 g (6 oz) self-raising flour, sifted

SALTED BRANDY CARAMEL
70 g (2½ oz) caster (superfine) sugar
60 g (2¼ oz) butter
125 ml (4 fl oz) thickened (whipping) cream
1–2 tablespoons brandy, to taste
Flaky sea salt, to taste

HACK THE RECIPE
Instead of making the ice-cream, buy a high-quality vanilla bean ice-cream or your favourite flavour to customise it.

This recipe is near and dear to my heart. It was the first one I attempted in the *MasterChef* kitchen, and I somehow ended up winning the challenge. It might surprise you now, but I was always a savoury cook; I never really understood desserts. I love how savoury food is open and has some leeway, whereas desserts are set and have to be done a certain way. The recipes are rigid, but because that's the case, if you follow it perfectly, the result should always be wonderful. This sandwich is made of koulourakia, my yiayia's Greek Easter biscuits, twirled into a circle, with fruity and savoury extra-virgin olive oil ice-cream. Then there's a wonderful brandy caramel drizzled all over for a salty-sweet finish. Hopefully it opens up your love for desserts as it did for me.

Pre-chill the bowl of an ice-cream machine and prepare an ice bath by filling a large bowl with ice cubes and water (see Notes). Preheat oven to 180°C (350°F) fan-forced and line a baking tray with baking paper.

To make the olive oil ice-cream, pour the cream and milk into a small saucepan over medium heat. Heat until it begins to steam (without boiling), then take off the heat. Place the sugar and eggs in a stand mixer with the whisk attachment and whisk until pale. Pour half the cream mixture over the egg mixture and whisk until combined. Return the mixture to the pan and place back over medium heat. Using a silicone spatula, stir until the mixture thickens and reaches 84°C (175°F) on a cook's thermometer (see Notes). Immediately take off the heat and pour through a fine sieve into a heatproof bowl. Carefully place the bowl in the ice bath so the bowl is sitting level on the ice cubes. Add a pinch of salt. Whisk in the oil until combined, then allow to cool. Transfer the mixture to the chilled ice-cream machine bowl and churn according to manufacturer's instructions. Place in the freezer until ice-cream consistency.

While the ice-cream churns and firms up, make the lemon koulourakia. Separate 1 egg, then place the egg yolk in the clean mixer with the whisk attachment, along with the butter, cream, sugar and lemon zest. Whisk until combined. Hand-whisk the separated egg white in a bowl, then gently whisk into the egg yolk mixture. Once combined, gradually add the flour a little at a time, until a soft, smooth and malleable dough forms. Roll the dough into a log, then cut into sixteen even pieces. Roll out each piece into a long, thin length. Join the ends of two pieces together, then twist them together lengthways, then shape into a circular wreath. Place on the

Notes

- If time is on your side, you can chill the ice-cream mixture in the fridge rather than using an ice bath.
- If you don't have a cook's thermometer to test the temperature of the cream mixture, if it coats the back of a spoon, it's ready.
- If you want to make a big batch of the koulourakia to eat separately, check out the recipe on page 123.
- Leftover ice-cream will keep in the freezer for up to 6 months.

prepared tray. Lightly whisk the remaining egg in a small bowl, then brush the egg wash over the wreath. Repeat with the remaining dough and egg wash to make twelve to sixteen wreaths in total. Bake for 12 minutes, or until golden. Take out of the oven and allow to cool.

While the koulourakia bake and cool, make the salted brandy caramel. Place the sugar and a dash of water in a small saucepan over medium–low heat. Stir until the sugar dissolves. Continue to cook, without stirring, until the sugar mixture is dark brown in colour. Dice the butter, then whisk into the sugar mixture. Once the butter melts, whisk in the cream until combined (be careful as it may spit). Whisk in the brandy, then take off the heat. Season with sea salt, then whisk until the brandy has emulsified into the caramel and it's a nice, thick consistency.

To serve, sandwich a generous scoop of the ice-cream between two biscuits and place on a serving plate. Repeat with the remaining ice-cream and biscuits, then drizzle the caramel sauce over the top.

RECIPES TO PREPARE WHILE YOU CHILL OUT

I'VE GOT SUNDAY FREE

THESE ARE THE RECIPES THAT GO BEYOND THE 2-HOUR MARK.

They're designed for lazy Sundays when you want to have a wholesome day at home, but also want to accomplish something. The best part about slower recipes is there is a little work at the start, a little work at the end, and a lot of feet up in between while the slow heat does all the work for you.

VILLAGE BREAD (V)

HORIATIKO PSOMI

Time
4 hours 20 minutes

MAKES 1 LOAF

2 teaspoons (7 g sachet) instant yeast (see Notes)
1 teaspoon caster (superfine) sugar or honey (see Notes)
390 ml (14 fl oz) warm water, plus extra 50 ml (1½ fl oz)
375 g (13 oz) bread flour (see Notes)
150 g (5½ oz) durum (semolina) wheat, plus extra for dusting
1 tablespoon olive oil
2 teaspoons salt
Ice cubes

Notes

- I recommend using an 'all-in-one' instant yeast and bread improver, or an instant baking yeast or bread machine yeast (depending on where you are in the world). Regular instant yeast works fine too.
- To make this bread vegan, use caster sugar instead of honey.
- If bread flour isn't available, swap for plain (all-purpose) flour.
- You can also bake the bread on a baking tray (still using the square of baking paper), if you prefer.

Horiatiko psomi is a rustic, village-style bread that involves little-to-no kneading or a stand mixer. This bread is close to my heart, as my yiayia would bake it religiously. We'd wake up after sleepovers at hers to the bread, smeared with butter and Vegemite. This loaf isn't meant to be the greatest bread you've ever had; it's just really, really good and doesn't take much effort. All you need is a bit of time. The secret to the excellent texture is the durum wheat, which gives it more bite, while retaining the softness. I use a casserole dish (Dutch oven) as it distributes the heat so well, but if you only have a baking tray, that's fine – it's how every Greek person would have done it back in the village.

Place the yeast, sugar or honey and warm water in a small bowl and give it a quick whisk. Sit for 5 minutes to activate the yeast (it'll begin to bubble at the top).

Place the flour and durum wheat in a large bowl and mix together.

Pour the yeast mixture over the flour mixture, along with the oil. Using a wooden spoon, mix together, then at the end, use clean hands to knead until all the remaining flour is incorporated. Cover the bowl with plastic wrap and place in a warm spot for 30 minutes, or until doubled in size.

Combine the salt and extra warm water, then add to the dough and knead for 30 seconds, or until combined. Shape into a square. Fold each side, lifting the bottom of a side up and over the middle of the dough. Cover again with plastic wrap, then rest in the warm spot for 1 hour.

Repeat the four-side fold and rest in the warm spot for 1 more hour, or until doubled in size.

Cut a square of baking paper. Allow the dough to fall out of the bowl onto a clean, dry benchtop. Using slightly wet hands, fold and shape the dough into a smooth oval shape. Place on the paper, then lower into a casserole dish (Dutch oven). Cover with a tea (dish) towel or lid and rest for 30 minutes.

Preheat oven to 220°C (425°F) fan-forced.

Using a small sieve, dust a thin layer of extra durum wheat over the dough. With a clean razor or serrated knife, carve a cross in the middle of the dough. (This allows the bread to get some height.) Add couple of ice cubes to the dish and close the lid again (or cover with foil). Bake for 30 minutes, then take off the lid and bake for a further 35–40 minutes, or until deep brown on top and around the side. Cool in the dish and once cool enough to touch, slice.

Time
3 hours 40 minutes

MEAT PASTA BAKE

PASTITSIO

SERVES 6–9

1 quantity Greek Bolognese (page 196)
500 g (1 lb 2 oz) pastitsio pasta no. 2 (see Note)

BECHAMEL SAUCE
100 g (3½ oz) butter
100 g (3½ oz) plain (all-purpose) flour
4 cups (1 litres) full-cream (whole) milk
2 eggs
2 egg yolks
¼ nutmeg
Salt, to taste

Note
Pastitsio pasta is long thick noodle with a hole through it. If you are unable to source it, bucatini, which is very similar, will work just as well.

TASTES EVEN BETTER THE NEXT DAY

The Greek lasagne. The structural heaven of pasta, rich bolognese and a creamy bechamel. The pastitsio is beloved, and really should be as popular as lasagne – it just needs better marketing. My mum would make this once a week growing up, then we would gorge on the leftovers every night until it ran out. As I have gotten older, it's become a staple in the freezer ready to go if a hangover ever makes an appearance. Reheated and covered in feta, this is as comforting as Greek food gets. Now, don't put too much pressure on yourself with the build; it takes time to learn, but no matter how it ends up in the tray, it'll come out tasting good.

Begin by cooking the bolognese.

While the bolognese is cooking, cook the pasta in a saucepan of boiling salted water following packet directions until just before al dente. Drain, then cool. Once cold enough to handle, arrange the pasta in a deep large baking tray. Try to have the pasta going lengthways so there are as few gaps as possible. The pasta will naturally stick to itself, so once all in, push down to help keep it connected.

To make the bechamel sauce, add the butter to same pan over high heat and melt, then whisk in the flour. Cook for 1–2 minutes. Pour in the milk, then whisk hard until the bechamel starts to thicken. (You want it to be thinner than a typical bechamel.) Turn off the heat and whisk in the eggs and egg yolks super quickly so as not scramble them. Finely grate in the nutmeg, then season with salt.

Preheat oven to 180°C (350°F) fan-forced.

Once the bolognese is done, pour it over the pasta in the tray and spread so it's even and as flat as possible. Gently pour the bechamel over the top (not lifting the pan too high as you pour to avoid disrupting the ragu and mixing them together). Using the back of a spoon, gently smooth the bechamel so it sits on top of the ragu as a separate, even layer. Bake for 40 minutes, or until a nice golden brown colour has covered most of the top. Take out of the oven, then give it 10 minutes resting to allow the bechamel to set a little bit before cutting into pieces to serve.

LAYERED SPANAKOPITA (V)

Time
2 hours 20 minutes

SERVES 8

2 leeks
1 bunch spring onions (scallions)
3 tablespoons dried oregano
½ nutmeg
800 g (1 lb 12 oz) baby spinach
1 bunch fresh dill
400 g (14 oz) feta cheese
3 eggs
¼ cup (30 g) dry (packaged) breadcrumbs
250 g (9 oz) filo pastry sheets, at room temperature (see Notes)
¼ cup (40 g) sesame seeds
Olive oil
Salt and cracked black pepper, to taste

Notes

- I recommend a chilled filo, like Antoniou Fillo Pastry, rather than frozen. If only frozen filo is available, remember to thaw completely before you begin the cook.
- Pre-cutting the top of the spanakopita makes it easier to cut individual serves after it's cooked without shattering the filo.

Spanakopita is my favourite Greek dish. Every Easter or Christmas, I would sneak pieces before we sat down, only to be full by the time it came to actually having lunch. My yiayia would make the filo fresh on the dining table, meticulously pulling it out bit by bit. As lovely as that is, it's time-consuming, so here is the next best thing. Instead of a coil, this is a lazier, more village style, but it still has the filo layers to give that classic bite and feel. Use this filling in pastry triangles or as a pasta shell filling too.

Place a large heavy-based saucepan over medium heat, then add 1 tablespoon oil. While the pan gets hot, thinly slice the leeks and spring onions. Add to the pan with 2 pinches of salt and sweat down for 5 minutes. Add another tablespoon oil in the middle of the pan, then add the oregano. Finely grate in the nutmeg and sizzle, without stirring, then stir it through for a minute.

In batches, add the spinach and for the last batch, take the pan off the heat and stir through until just wilted. (You don't want the spinach to overcook.)

Finely chop the dill and add to the pan. Crumble in the feta. Add the eggs. Stir through. Add a big pinch of salt and a few cracks pepper. If the filling is a bit wet, just give it a good mix. (The filo will absorb most of the liquid.)

Preheat oven to 190°C (375°F) fan-forced.

Sprinkle breadcrumbs over the base of a deep baking tray (to ensure there's no soggy bottom). Lay four filo sheets over the breadcrumbs to cover, allowing one-quarter of each sheet to hang over the tray edges so there's overhang on all sides. Lightly brush the filo with oil. Lay two sheets straight down the middle to create a solid base, brushing with oil between each one.

Working with a quarter of the filling, spoon it over the filo in three thin logs lengthways. Lay two filo sheets on top, brushing each one with oil and pushing down in between the filling, so it looks like three speed bumps in rows. Working with another quarter of the filling, spoon over three more logs of filling into the gaps created so you end up with a flat top. Place a couple more filo sheets on top, brushing each one with oil.

Repeat layering once more with the remaining filling and more filo. Finish with a couple of filo sheets, brushing with oil. Using the brush, push the overhanging filo up over the top. Using a serrated knife, cut just through the top layer into eight squares (see Notes). Scatter the sesame seeds over the top.

Bake for 1 hour 30–1 hour 40 minutes, or until golden. Set aside until cool to the touch, then cut all the way through the pieces to serve.

OREGANO LAMB SHOULDER

Time
7 hours 15 minutes

SERVES 8–10

2 kg (4 lb 8 oz) lamb shoulder, bone in
20 g (¾ oz) fresh oregano leaves
4 garlic cloves
2 lemons
2 tablespoons dried oregano
⅓ cup (80 ml) olive oil
1 tablespoon salt
Flaky sea salt, to taste

Note
This lamb is delicious served with the Oven-roasted potatoes (page 160) and/or the Turkish grain salad (page 106).

This dish is the one that gets cooked the most by my followers, and boy, do they like to tell me how much they love it. It's a foolproof recipe that never lets you down. Perfect for Easter or Christmas, it brings together the classic Greek flavours that I rely on, because if it ain't broke ... Cooked with a mixture of garlic, lemon, olive oil and lots of oregano, the lamb is fragrant, zesty and just falls apart. I have spent a few years trying to get the cook time right, and I think I have nailed it. The lamb comes out blushing every time, and it's very beginner friendly to cook. Just put together the marinade, lamb in the oven and walk away – slow-cooked food doesn't get any better.

Preheat oven to 150°C (300°F) fan-forced.

Prep the lamb shoulder by using a sharp knife to remove any excess fat. (I like to remove most of the fat, so all that remains is a very thin layer you can see the lamb flesh through. This step is very important, so don't skip it.) Using the knife, stab holes all over the lamb to make pockets for the marinade to get into, being careful not to hit the bone.

Finely chop the oregano leaves and mince the garlic, and place both on a large baking tray. Finely grate the zest of both lemons over the top. Halve 1 lemon and squeeze the juice into the tray. Add the dried oregano, oil and salt. Using your fingers, bring it together until you have a bright green marinade. Add the lamb and rub in the marinade until it's covered, pushing the marinade into the knife holes. Using a tablespoon, add ⅓ cup (80 ml) water to the tray, placing about 1 tablespoon in each corner. Cover with foil and roast for 2 hours.

Take the tray out of the oven and baste the lamb with the tray juices. Reduce oven to 130°C (250°F) fan-forced, cover the tray again, then return it to the oven for a further 3 hours 30 minutes.

Remove the foil and baste again with the tray juices. Roast, uncovered, for a further 30 minutes. Take out of the oven, cover the tray again and rest for at least 30 minutes.

When ready to serve, shred the lamb using a couple of forks or with clean hands (which is what I prefer). The lamb should tear easily into pieces. Roll the meat through the tray juices so it's covered with the cooked marinade.

Cut the remaining lemon into wedges. Serve the lamb sprinkled with sea salt and the lemon wedges to squeeze over the top right before eating.

RED BEEF STEW

Time
3 hours 30 minutes

SERVES 4

KOKKINISTO

2 tablespoons olive oil
800 g (1 lb 12 oz) gravy beef
1 large brown onion
1 large red onion
1 carrot
3 garlic cloves
1 tablespoon dried oregano
1 tablespoon ground allspice
2 teaspoons ground paprika
2 teaspoons ground cinnamon
½ teaspoon chilli flakes
¼ teaspoon ground cloves
70 g (2½ oz) tomato paste (concentrated purée)
1 cup (250 ml) red wine
400 g (14 oz) tin diced tomatoes
3 fresh bay leaves
Salt and cracked black pepper, to taste
Steamed rice or cooked pasta, to serve (optional)

Note
This stew will keep in an airtight container in the fridge for up to 3 days or in the freezer for up to 6 months.

TASTES EVEN BETTER THE NEXT DAY

I recommend placing yourself in front of a Greek person and watching their eyes light up when they find out you're serving kokkinisto. This is the most popular stew across the islands and mainland, and depending on where you go, it's always a bit different. Whether it be chicken or beef, or the different spices used, each family has their own version passed down from generation to generation. My kokkinisto comes from my mum, which came from Mum's mum and so on. Our version is heavy on allspice, and includes paprika and cinnamon, as well as chilli flakes, which is very un-Greek, but my mum added it in years ago. It just gives the kokkinisto this light spice that helps bring out all the other spices. Serve it on pasta or rice, it's the winter stew that never disappoints.

Place a heavy-based saucepan over high heat, then add half the oil. While the pan gets hot enough to sear, cut the beef into thick cubes. Add half the beef to the hot pan and brown on one side, then turn and brown on the other side. You will know the beef is seared when it easily pulls away from the base of the pan. Transfer the beef to a plate, then repeat with the remaining oil and beef, then transfer to the plate.

While the beef sears, finely dice the brown and red onions, and carrot.

Reduce heat to low. Add the onion and carrot to the pan. Sauté with a big pinch of salt for 8–10 minutes, adding a dash of water if it starts to burn.

While the vegetables sauté, thinly slice the garlic and measure out the spices.

Add the garlic, spices and tomato paste, and mix for a minute to cook out any bitterness. Increase heat to high. Add wine to deglaze the pan, using a wooden spoon to scrape the base of the pan. Cook until reduced by three-quarters.

Add the tomatoes, along with an empty tin's worth of water (400 ml/14 fl oz). Add the beef and bay leaves. Mix everything in. Season with salt and pepper, and bring up to a gentle simmer. Once simmering, reduce heat to very low, cover with the lid and bubble away for 2 hours.

Remove the lid, season with salt and gently simmer and bubble away, uncovered, for a further 45 minutes, stirring a couple of times as it reduces to make sure it doesn't get stuck on the base of the pan.

Season with salt if it needs it and remove the bay leaves. Serve with rice or pasta, if you like.

Time
2 hours 45 minutes

GREEK BOLOGNESE

SERVES 6

MAKARONIA ME KIMA

100 g (3½ oz) dried spaghetti per serve (see Notes)
20 g (¾ oz) kefalograviera cheese (see Notes)

BOLOGNESE
2 tablespoons olive oil, plus extra if needed
500 g (1 lb 2 oz) minced (ground) beef
500 g (1 lb 2 oz) minced (ground) pork
2 celery stalks
2 carrots
2 brown onions
6 garlic cloves
1 tablespoon ground allspice
2 teaspoons ground cinnamon
¼ teaspoon ground cloves
70 g (2½ oz) tomato paste (concentrated purée)
1 cup (250 ml) red wine
800 g (1 lb 12 oz) tin diced tomatoes
2 fresh or dried bay leaves
Salt, to taste

Bolognese is universally loved, so it shouldn't surprise you that the Greek version is a nostalgic favourite. It's not very hands-on, and just relies on building flavour before letting it simmer away. Along with pastitsio (page 189), Greek kids hang out for this dish. Yiayia would make batches of it all the time, to thaw and heat up when all the cousins came over. The smell takes over the entire house – the combination of allspice, cinnamon and clove coming together in an aromatic, addictive meat sauce. I have used kefalograviera on top to finish, but honestly, you can also use the cheapest grated parmesan you can find, just like my yiayia did.

To make the bolognese, place a large saucepan over high heat, then add the oil. Once the pan is hot, add the beef. Using a wooden spoon or spatula, push down on the beef (don't break it up). Sizzle, without stirring, for 5 minutes, or until deeply caramelised and charred. Take out of the pan and set aside on a plate. Repeat with the pork, adding a little extra oil if the pan looks dry.

While the meat caramelises, cut the celery, carrots, onions and garlic into medium-sized pieces and transfer to a food processor. Blitz until it's a slushy consistency. Add 2 tablespoons water if it needs help blending.

Once the pork has been removed from the pan, add the blitzed vegetables to the pan with the meaty oil. Add 2 teaspoons salt. Sauté, stirring every so often, for 7 minutes. Mix through the spices and cook for a minute. Add the tomato paste and cook, stirring, for 1 more minute. Pour in the wine and cook out completely – about 5 minutes. (You want a relatively dry base at the end.)

TASTES EVEN BETTER THE NEXT DAY

Notes

- This recipe makes enough bolognese for six serves, but adjust the amount of pasta depending on how many serves you need. The leftover bolognese will keep in an airtight container in the fridge for up to 3 days or in the freezer for up to 6 months.
- If kefalograviera is hard to find, swap for parmesan cheese.

Return the meat to the pan and using a wooden spoon, break down into small pieces. Mix through and cook for a minute. Add the tomatoes, along with an empty tin's worth of water (800 ml/28 fl oz). Add the bay leaves, season with salt and bring to a simmer. Reduce heat to low until it's gently bubbling. Gently simmer for 2 hours, giving it a mix now and again closer to the end of the cook, so nothing burns on the bottom. Season with salt, if it needs it. Remove the bay leaves.

When the bolognese is nearly done, bring a saucepan of salted water to a rolling boil over high heat. Cook the pasta following packet directions until al dente. Drain.

When ready to plate, divide the pasta among serving plates, top with the bolognese, then finish by grating the cheese over the top.

POACHED QUINCE (VE)

Time
5 hours

SERVES 4

1 lemon
500 g (1 lb 2 oz) caster (superfine) sugar
6 star anise
6 whole cloves
3 dried bay leaves
1 cinnamon stick
4 quinces

Notes

- A cartouche is a piece of baking paper used as a false lid in cooking. It allows everything to cook thoroughly but gently underneath without using a lid, which traps the heat. To create one, grab a square of baking paper and cut into a circle to fit the pan. Cut a couple of little holes in it to allow the heat and air to distribute, and place in the pan so it's floating on top of the quinces.
- Store the poached quince in the poaching liquid in an airtight container in the fridge for up to a week.

Quince is one of the most important fruits to Greek people, from ancient to medieval to modern times. It was used for medicinal purposes, preserved in honey, as well being included in celebrations, particularly weddings. It's an ingredient that often scares people, I think. It's also forgotten about, because of the time-consuming cooking time, but I implore you to give this a go. The poached ruby red quince is a thing of beauty and the flavour you get is like no other fruit in the world. My recipe could not be easier, and it just needs some time to slowly cook – it's a you-sitting-on-the-couch-while-it-bubbles-away-in-the-background recipe. Enjoy the poached fruit with Greek-style yoghurt or vanilla ice-cream and Cinnamon crumble (page 217). The by-product is a quince syrup that is my favourite to use in cocktails or on top of ice-cream. Quince is available only in winter, so when you see it hit the shelves, take advantage of this sacred fruit.

Using a peeler, cut all the peel off the lemon until it's bare. Add the lemon peel to a large saucepan. Halve the lemon and squeeze in the juice of both halves. Add the remaining ingredients, except the quinces, and 8 cups (2 litres) water. Bring to a simmer over medium heat.

While the poaching liquid comes to a simmer, prep the quinces by peeling off the skin. Using a sharp knife, cut into quarters, then cut the middle core out of each quarter. (It's important to get out all or most of the core as it will be gritty once cooked.) As you've cut each piece, immediately add it to the poaching liquid (as it will oxidise very fast).

Once all the quince is in the poaching liquid, place a cartouche (see Notes) on top and once it comes back to a gentle simmer, reduce heat to low and let it gently bubble away for 3 hours 30 minutes–4 hours, or until the quince becomes a blushing ruby red colour, but still holds its shape. (If you cook quince for too long it will fall apart, so check the progress as it bubbles away.) Take off the heat and rest for a minimum of 30 minutes, or preferably 1 hour.

Using a slotted spoon, transfer the poached quince to a serving bowl to serve.

If you want to make the quince syrup, place the poaching liquid back over medium heat and reduce it down into a thicker syrup. Once it has thickened to the point where you can pick it up with a spoon and when poured back in, it holds its shape a little, take off the heat. You don't want it too thick, as the syrup will thicken as it cools down. Cool, then strain into a jar and store in the fridge for up to a year.

LEMON TIRAMISU

Time
3 hours

SERVES 12

LEMON SYRUP
1 cup (220 g) caster (superfine) sugar
2 lemons
2 tablespoons limoncello

CREAM
3 eggs
1 lemon
500 g (1 lb 2 oz) chilled mascarpone
1 tablespoon vanilla extract
80 g (2¾ oz) caster (superfine) sugar
Salt, to taste

BUILD
50 g (1¾ oz) dehydrated blood orange or orange wheels (see Notes)
380 g (13½ oz) savoiardi (lady finger biscuits)

Notes

- Find dehydrated orange wheels at most supermarkets. Choose blood orange for a deeper colour (the flavour will be very similar).
- Make sure the orange wheels are completely dry and dehydrated before you blitz them or it won't work.

Tiramisu is a favourite for good reason. It's not Greek, but Italy isn't very far away. The classic is wonderful, but I think a great way to showcase the humble lemon is in this dessert. This is screaming for you to make it during summer, as it's brighter and lighter than the coffee and chocolate version. A lot of different online recipes tend to add lemon curd as one of the layers, but for me, that's a lot of soft textures and really, it become a hassle to make. So, I have opted for layering dehydrated orange dust, which is a lot easier to achieve, and adds wonderful colour. If you want to pop in lemon curd, I won't stop you, but I think this is perfect the way it is.

To make the lemon syrup, place the sugar and 1 cup (250 ml) water in a saucepan. Using a peeler, cut all the peel off the lemons until they're bare. Add the lemon peel to the pan and bring to a gentle simmer over medium–low heat, stirring as it heats up. Simmer for 10 minutes, or until the syrup has a strong lemon taste. Take off the heat.

While the sugar mixture is simmering, halve the lemons and squeeze the juice of all halves. Strain into a bowl to catch any large chunks and pips. Discard the solids.

Stir the lemon juice, limoncello and 2 cups (500 ml) water into the sugar mixture. Cool completely.

To make the cream, separate the eggs, placing the yolks in a large bowl. Finely grate in the zest of the lemon over the yolks. Add the mascarpone and vanilla. Whip until slightly thickened and increased in volume. (Be careful not to over-whip. It should hold its shape when you pull out the whisk.) In a separate bowl, whip the egg whites, sugar and a pinch of salt until soft peaks form. In two batches, fold the egg white mixture into the mascarpone mixture until incorporated. Place in the fridge for 2 hours, or until ready to assemble.

Place the orange wheels in a high-powdered blender or food processor and blitz to a fine powder (see Notes).

To build the tiramisu, grab a deep baking tray. One at a time, dunk the lady fingers in the lemon syrup, holding down in the syrup for 1 second on each side (any longer and the biscuit will crumble into the syrup), then lay them lengthways in a single layer to cover the base of the tray. Spread half the cream over the top and smooth out so it's even. Top with half the orange dust by pouring it into a sieve over the tray and smacking the sieve to dust all over. Repeat layering with the remaining biscuits and cream, finishing with the remaining orange dust to serve.

WHOLE ORANGE FILO CAKE

Time
2 hours 10 minutes

SERVES 9

PORTOKALOPITA

2 large oranges
250 g (9 oz) chilled filo pastry sheets (see Notes)
6 whole cloves
3 whole star anise
1 cinnamon stick
1¼ cups (275 g) caster (superfine) sugar
Butter, for greasing
Plain (all-purpose) flour, for dusting
2 eggs
½ cup (125 ml) full-cream (whole) milk
100 ml (3½ fl oz) extra-virgin olive oil (see Notes)
1 teaspoon bicarbonate of soda (baking soda)
1 teaspoon baking powder
Chantilly cream, to serve (page 71)

Notes

- I recommend a chilled filo, like Antoniou Fillo Pastry, rather than frozen. If only frozen filo is available, remember to thaw so it's just chilled before you begin the cook.
- Olive oil is traditional for this recipe, but any neutral oil will work fine.
- When testing that the cake is ready, don't worry about poking holes through the filo with the skewer as you will need holes for the syrup anyway.

Portokalopita is one of the most interesting cakes, because it uses filo pastry instead of flour for its structure. This creates incredibly soft, moist layers that just melt in your mouth. Portokalopita translates to 'orange pie.' It's a real celebration of orange; a whole orange gets boiled, then blitzed with the wet ingredients. My version isn't as sweet as portokalopita I've had before. It's more floral, with just the right amount of sweetness, so it doesn't feel too rich and leaves you wanting more. Plus, it's also a smaller version of the classic, massive trays the cake is usually baked in. You can easily double this recipe for a big tray, if you like – just increase the cooking time a bit and keep an eye on it.

Preheat oven to 100°C (200°F) fan-forced.

Place 1 orange in a saucepan and cover with water. Bring to the boil over high heat, then cover with the lid and cook for 1 hour.

Meanwhile, place the filo on a baking tray. From one short end, use clean, dry hands to drag the pastry until it forms an accordion-like shape, squishing the sheets together. Bake for 1 hour, or until dried and crisp. Take out of the oven.

While the orange boils and the filo bakes, finely grate the zest of the remaining orange into a bowl, then halve the orange and squeeze the juice into a small jug. Place the cloves, star anise, cinnamon, 175 g (6 oz) sugar and 175 ml (2¼ fl oz) water in a saucepan and bring to the boil over medium heat. Cook, stirring, for 2 minutes. Take off the heat. Mix in the juice. Transfer the syrup to a heatproof bowl and place in the fridge to chill until required.

Increase oven to 160°C (325°F) fan-forced. Grease a 22.5 cm (8½ in) square cake pan with butter, then dust with flour, shaking out excess.

Roughly chop the boiled orange. Place in a food processor. Lightly whisk the eggs in a small bowl, then add to the processor, along with the zest, milk, oil, bicarb, baking powder and remaining 100 g (3½ oz) sugar. Process until as smooth as possible. Transfer the batter to a large bowl. Using clean, dry hands, break the filo into shards over the batter. Mix in with a wooden spoon.

Pour the batter into prepared pan. Bake for 40–45 minutes, or until a skewer inserted into the middle comes out clean and the top is deep golden (see Notes).

As the cake goes in the oven, place the syrup in the freezer to get super cold.

Take the cake out of the oven. Poke all over with a skewer. Slowly pour the syrup over the top. Let it absorb for a few minutes, then serve with Chantilly.

CHOCOLATE CAKE

Time
2 hours 20 minutes

SERVES 20

SOKOLATOPITA

Unsalted butter, for greasing
360 g (12¾ oz) plain (all-purpose) flour
115 g (4 oz) unsweetened cocoa powder
2 teaspoons baking powder
1½ teaspoons bicarbonate of soda (baking soda)
1½ teaspoons salt
275 g (9¾ oz) caster (superfine) sugar
200 g (7 oz) soft light brown sugar
3 eggs
330 g (11½ oz) buttermilk
155 g (5½ oz) olive oil
220 g (7¾ oz) sour cream
1 tablespoon vanilla extract

WHIPPED CHOCOLATE GANACHE
720 g (1 lb 10 oz) milk chocolate
280 ml (6 fl oz) thickened (whipping) cream, plus a little extra for troubleshooting
Flaky sea salt, to taste

SYRUP
300 g (10½ oz) caster (superfine) sugar
50 g (1¾ oz) unsweetened cocoa powder
¼ cup (60 ml) Licor 43 (see Notes)

Notes

- Licor 43 is a Spanish liqueur available at bottle shops. If not available, any spice-driven liqueur is great. Or feel free to omit the alcohol or swap for 1 tablespoon vanilla extract.
- Blitzing extra cream into the ganache with a hand-held blender also works if it has separated.

Sokolatopita is a cake that tends to come out for celebrations in Greece, and everyone has their own version. Truly, if you scour the internet, not one family's recipe will be the same. Mine is no exception, as it takes a more modern approach to the cake, using buttermilk and sour cream (not like the classic), but it just combines so well with the olive oil. It leaves a moist, melt-in-your-mouth finish. The one thing Greek chocolate cakes do have in common is being drenched in a chocolate syrup, as is always the way with Greek cakes. This recipe can be done without the syrup (I know some of you won't want it) and it's been designed for both ways, but I do recommend sticking with the syrup as it takes this dessert to another level and sets it apart from other chocolate cakes. The addition of whipped chocolate ganache is dreamy, and honestly, once you've mastered it, you'll top all your baked goods with it.

To make the whipped chocolate ganache, finely chop the chocolate and place in a heatproof bowl. Pour the thickened cream into a saucepan and bring to the boil over medium heat (you want it very hot and bubbling). Pour the hot cream over the chocolate, place a tea (dish) towel over the bowl and leave for 5 minutes.

Take off the tea towel and stir with a spoon to bring the ganache together. (If the ganache still has lumps of chocolate, pour in a dash of extra thickened cream. Using a hand-held blender, blitz until smooth; see Notes.) Add a couple of pinches of flaky sea salt. Once the ganache is smooth and velvety, cover the surface with plastic wrap (to stop a skin forming). Place in the fridge for 1 hour to chill.

While the ganache chills, make the syrup the cake will get drenched in. Place the caster sugar, cocoa and 300 ml (10½ fl oz) water in a saucepan over high heat. Using a whisk, bring together until combined and the mixture comes to the boil. Take off the heat and whisk in the liqueur. Pour the syrup into a heatproof jug and place in the fridge until completely chilled.

Preheat oven to 180°C (350°F) fan-forced.

Place a little butter in a small microwave-safe bowl and microwave until melted. Grease a deep baking tray (mine is 27 × 38 cm/11 × 15 in) with the melted butter. (This is just your insurance, so you can easily cut the cake straight from the tray.) Using paper towel, wipe to remove any puddles of excess butter.

Whisk together the flour, cocoa, baking powder, bicarb and salt in a large bowl. In a separate bowl, whisk together the sugars, eggs, buttermilk, oil, sour cream and vanilla until you have a smooth, light brown liquid. Pour the wet mixture over the dry mixture. Using the whisk, gently fold together until well combined. Pour the batter into the prepared tray and smooth the surface so it's flat across the top. Bake for 30–35 minutes, or until a skewer inserted into the middle comes out clean. (You will also notice the sides of the cake begin to peel away from the tray, which is a great sign.)

Using the skewer, poke holes all over the cake, then pour the cold syrup all over the hot cake, starting from the edges and working your way in, and making sure to pour into all the holes and all over the top of the cake. Stand the cake for 1 hour to swim in the syrup and soak it up.

While the cake soaks, use electric beaters to whisk the ganache until smooth, light and fluffy. This will take a second if it's very cold, but just keep whisking until it becomes pale in colour.

Top the cake with a layer of whipped ganache, creating ripples with a plastic spatula. If not eating straight away, place in the fridge until ready to serve. Let it come to room temperature before serving.

CUSTARD FILO PIE

Time
5 hours

SERVES 20–24

GALAKTOBOUREKO

200 g (7 oz) unsalted butter
375 g (13 oz) chilled filo pastry sheets (see Notes)
6 eggs
8 cups (2 litres) full-cream (whole) milk
1 cup (220 g) caster (superfine) sugar
1 cup (180 g) durum (semolina) wheat
25 g (1 oz) vanilla sugar

SYRUP
2 cups (440 g) caster (superfine) sugar
2 cinnamon sticks
2 lemon slices
2 tablespoons honey

Notes

- I recommend a chilled filo, like Antoniou Fillo Pastry, rather than frozen. If only frozen filo is available, remember to thaw so it's just chilled before you begin the cook.
- When making the custard, be careful not to let the milk come to a simmer, as it will burn on the bottom. Constant stirring will also help make sure this doesn't happen.
- Pre-cutting the top of the pie makes it easier to cut individual serves after it's cooked without shattering the filo.
- Pouring cold syrup over super-hot filo 'shocks' the pastry. The temperature change creates a really flaky, crunchy top.

TASTES EVEN BETTER THE NEXT DAY

Every family member makes a certain dish the best. In my family, it's my mum's galaktoboureko. 'Galactic booty call' as my dad pronounces it. This is the quintessential Greek dessert. Custard, filo and syrup – the holy trinity of Greek desserts. This is Mum's recipe verbatim; I wouldn't change a thing. It might seem a lot to handle, but it uses simple ingredients, and once it's in the oven, you get to kick back before pouring the syrup on top.

Preheat oven to 150°C (300°F) fan-forced.

Place the butter in a small microwave-safe bowl and microwave until melted. Lay 1 filo sheet down in the middle of a large deep baking tray. Brush the filo with some butter. Lay another filo sheet in the tray with one-quarter of the sheet overhanging one side. Brush with butter. Repeat with 3 more sheets, laying each one so it's overhanging a different side and brushing with butter. Repeat this process four more times with sixteen more filo sheets and butter. Cover the remaining filo with a tea (dish) towel so it doesn't dry out.

Whisk the eggs in a bowl. Place the milk and caster sugar in a large saucepan over medium–high heat (see Notes). Once steaming, slowly pour in the semolina. Whisk until incorporated, then whisk in the vanilla sugar. Reduce heat to medium, swap the whisk for a wooden spoon or rubber spatula and stir for 8–10 minutes, or until nice and thick, and resembles a thick pouring cream. Reduce heat to very low. In three batches, pour in the egg, making sure to stir in very fast so as to not curdle the eggs. Once the eggs are incorporated, take off the heat and keep stirring for 2 minutes (it will continue to cook).

Pour the custard into the tray over the filo, making sure not to pour any over the overhanging filo. Fold the overhanging filo over the custard, brushing with butter if it's a bit dry. Arrange the remaining filo on top in the middle of the tray, brushing between each sheet as you layer. Roll in the edges to create a filo border and brush the border and top with butter. Using a serrated knife, gently cut a diamond pattern just through the top layer of filo (see Notes). Bake for 3 hours, checking at the 2 hour 30 minute-mark to make sure it's getting lovely colour but not burning. (Cover with foil if needed.)

Meanwhile, make the syrup. Place all the ingredients and 2 cups (500 ml) water in a saucepan over medium–low heat. Bring to a gentle simmer. Cook for 15 minutes, then pour into a heatproof bowl. Place in the fridge to chill.

Once the pie is cooked, immediately pour the cold syrup over the top, allowing it to bubble all over (see Notes). Stand for at least 1 hour to help the pie set (if not, the custard will fall apart), then serve.

RECIPES THAT NEED TO RELAX

I'VE GOT OVERNIGHT

THESE ARE THE RECIPES THAT DO THE WORK WHILE YOU SLEEP.

These dishes need to relax just like you – whether it be to set, to drain or to marinate in flavour. The result is usually something pretty special, and all that was required was for you to hit the hay to make it happen.

Time
15 minutes
(+ overnight draining)

TZATZIKI (V)

SERVES 4–6
(AS A STARTER)

2 Lebanese (short) cucumbers
1 kg (2 lb 4 oz) Greek-style yoghurt
1 bunch fresh dill
4 garlic cloves
1 small lemon
¼ cup (60 ml) extra-virgin olive oil, plus extra for drizzling
Salt, to taste
Bread or crackers, to serve

Notes

- To make this dip vegan, swap the Greek-style yoghurt for unsweetened coconut yoghurt.
- If muslin is hard to source, large coffee filter paper will also work, or do it like an old-school Greek and add the yoghurt to a clean, thin tea (dish) towel and let it hang over a bowl to drip.
- Short on time? You can drain the cucumber and yoghurt for a minimum of 3 hours, but overnight works best for proper tzatziki.
- Tzatziki is best served fresh, but leftovers will keep in an airtight container in the fridge for up to 5 days.

Tzatziki should be two things: thick, and full of so much garlic that it's almost offensive. My mum's tip that I live by, because it's served me so well, is wrapping the grated cucumber and yoghurt in muslin (cheesecloth) and letting all the liquid drip out overnight. It just means the dip remains thick and not watery. You should try to drag a cracker through it – the cracker almost breaks because it's so thick. Serve up this beauty of a dip with lamb or any cooked protein and even potatoes – it goes with everything.

Place a piece of muslin (cheesecloth) into a sieve and set over a large bowl (see Notes). Grate the cucumbers on top of the muslin, then pour the yoghurt on top. Using an elastic band, tie the muslin tight at the top and place in the fridge overnight to drain.

Gently squeeze out any excess liquid, pressing into the sides of the muslin. Transfer the cucumber and yoghurt to a clean large bowl. Discard the liquid (or water your plants with it). Finely chop the dill and mince the garlic, and add both to the bowl. Finely grate in the zest of the lemon, then halve the lemon and squeeze in the juice of both halves. Pour in the oil, season with salt, then mix together with a spoon.

Spoon the tzatziki into a serving bowl, drizzle with extra oil and enjoy with bread or crackers.

BEETROOT TZATZIKI (V)

Time
25 minutes
(+ overnight draining)

SERVES 4–6
(AS A STARTER)

- 1 Lebanese (short) cucumber
- 500 g (1 lb 2 oz) Greek-style yoghurt
- 250 g (9 oz) cooked beetroot (beet)
- 20 g (¾ oz) fresh mint leaves, plus extra handful for garnishing
- 15 g (½ oz) fresh dill
- 3 garlic cloves
- ¼ cup (60 ml) extra-virgin olive oil
- 1 long pickled pepper (store-bought or for homemade, see page 226)
- 1 tablespoon baby capers
- Salt, to taste
- Bread or crackers, to serve

Notes

- To make this dip vegan, swap the Greek-style yoghurt for unsweetened coconut yoghurt.
- If muslin is hard to source, large coffee filter paper will also work, or do it like an old-school Greek and add the yoghurt to a clean, thin tea (dish) towel and let it hang over a bowl to drip.
- Short on time? You can drain the cucumber and yoghurt for a minimum of 3 hours, but overnight works best for proper tzatziki.

This is my entertaining tzatziki. This plate has the 'eye appeal' that just hits you straight away. The light sweetness of the beetroot with the fragrant mint take this dip to a different place. It gives the plate such a brightness, made to kick off a dinner party. The bright purply-pink makes it a gorg centrepiece to hold down your starters.

Place a piece of muslin (cheesecloth) into a sieve and set over a large bowl (see Notes). Grate the cucumber on top of the muslin, then pour the yoghurt on top. Using an elastic band, tie the muslin tight at the top and place in the fridge overnight to drain.

Gently squeeze out any excess liquid, pressing into the sides of the muslin. Transfer the cucumber and yoghurt to a clean large bowl. Discard the liquid (or water your plants with it).

Grate the beetroot into a sieve set over a separate bowl to drain.

Finely chop the mint and dill, and add to the yoghurt mixture, along with the beetroot. Mince the garlic and add to the bowl, along with 1 tablespoon oil. Season with salt (go hard here, it can handle it). Mix together with a spoon. You'll end up with a gorgeous pink/purple colour.

Spread the beetroot tzatziki over a large serving plate, creating a small moat through the middle with the back of the spoon. Roughly chop the pickled pepper, capers and extra mint together, then scatter the mixture over the tzatziki. Cover with the remaining 2 tablespoons oil. Enjoy with bread or crackers.

CHICKEN MARBELLA LA GRECA

Time
1 hour 10 minutes
(+ 8 hours brining)

SERVES 2

3 garlic cloves
6 medjool dates
¼ cup (60 ml) red wine vinegar
1 tablespoon honey
¼ cup (50 g) baby capers, plus 1 tablespoon caper brine
1 cup (250 ml) white wine
100 g (3½ oz) pitted kalamata olives
2 chicken marylands (leg quarters), thighs and drumsticks separated
Olive oil
Salt, to taste
Steamed rice, to serve

Notes

- If the chicken isn't mostly covered by the brine, add some water to do so – you shouldn't need more than ½ cup (125 ml).
- If you don't have a flameproof baking dish, don't worry. You can roast in a normal baking dish, then to make the gravy, pour the sauce mixture into a saucepan.
- When grilling the chicken, don't be scared to take it to the edge, as the brine will have kept the meat juicy. It should only take 3–5 minutes, depending on the oven strength, so stay close by and watch it.

Chicken Marbella is not Greek, it's never been Greek. It's actually a classic French recipe that featured in *The Silver Palate Cookbook*. This book was pioneering in how it taught Americans, and now the world, about French cooking. I love the recipe, because it is one of the easiest ways to achieve super juicy chicken as a home cook. It already hints at a Mediterranean feel, but I have swapped prunes for dates, sugar for honey and green olives for kalamata olives to turn it la Greca. This dish is a cross-section of sweet and savoury. The glossy sauce you end up with and the fall-apart chicken alone make this recipe worth trying. Honestly, it's not very hands-on either. A lot of the work is done by the brine while you sleep or go about your day. Feel free to add a side of blanched broccolini like my partner and I do. Begin this recipe the night before. (Alternatively, in the morning before work for dinner that night.)

Mince the garlic and place in a bowl. Pit the dates, then cut into quarters. Add to the bowl, along with the vinegar, honey, capers, caper brine, wine and olives. Season with salt. Mix together. Add the chicken, making sure it's sitting snugly in the brine and is at least mostly covered (see Notes). Cover with the lid or plastic wrap and place in the fridge for a minimum of 8 hours.

Preheat oven to 180°C (350°F) fan-forced.

Remove the bowl from the fridge and pour the contents into a flameproof baking dish (see Notes) and evenly spread out the mixture, with the chicken poking through, skin-side up. Roast, covered with foil, for 30 minutes.

Take the dish out of the oven and switch the oven to grill (broiler) on the highest temperature. Drizzle a little oil over the chicken skin. (This helps the skin char evenly.) Place under the grill and cook until the skin is deeply charred and caramelised (see Notes).

Take the dish out of the oven and transfer the chicken to a plate to rest. Using the same dish or a saucepan (see Notes), place over high heat and cook for about 8 minutes, or until reduced and thickened into a glossy gravy of your preferred consistency.

Pour the sauce, including all the olives, capers and dates, over the chicken and serve it up with rice to soak up all that goodness.

YOGHURT, HONEY AND CINNAMON CRUMBLE

Time
45 minutes
(+ overnight draining)

SERVES 4–6

YIAOURTI ME MELI

500 g (1 lb 2 oz) Greek-style yoghurt
100 g (3½ oz) Greek honey (see Notes)

CINNAMON CRUMBLE
⅓ cup (50 g) plain (all-purpose) flour
50 g (1¾ oz) caster (superfine) sugar
2 teaspoons ground cinnamon
50 g (1¾ oz) salted butter

Notes

- Greek honey is needed to replicate how this plate is served in Greece. Find it at specialty Mediterranean grocers. Alternatively, use a high-quality honey.
- If muslin is hard to source, large coffee filter paper will also work, or do it like an old-school Greek and add the yoghurt to a clean, thin tea (dish) towel and let it hang over a bowl to drip.

Greeks aren't actually known for after-dinner desserts. A lot of the sweet recipes from this book are treats you'd normally eat during the day, bought from a Greek bakery. After-dinner consists of fresh-cut watermelon or this incredibly simple plate of yoghurt and honey. The plate of cheesy, tangy yoghurt has a layer of Greek honey over the top and is sometimes topped with various nuts. As I have a nut allergy, I have paired this with my no-fail crumble. Spiced with cinnamon, it's a crumble made of equal parts sugar, flour and butter, and is great for sprinkling on top of sweet fruit-based desserts and yoghurt.

Place a piece of muslin (cheesecloth) in a sieve and set over a large bowl (see Notes). Spoon in the yoghurt. Using an elastic band, tie the muslin tight at the top and place in the fridge overnight to drain.

The next day, preheat oven to 180°C (350°F) fan-forced.

To make the cinnamon crumble, place the flour, sugar and cinnamon in a food processor and blitz together. Cube the butter, then add to the processor and pulse until a sandy texture is achieved. Spread the mixture over a small baking tray and bake for 10 minutes.

Give the crumble a mix, then bake for 10 more minutes. Give it another stir and bake for another 10 minutes (a total of 30 minutes oven time). Take the tray out of the oven and cool for 5 minutes.

When ready to serve, remove the sieve from the fridge and gently squeeze out any excess liquid, pressing into the sides of the muslin. Transfer the yoghurt to a clean bowl. Discard the liquid (or water your plants with it).

To plate, spoon the drained yoghurt onto a deep serving plate, drizzle with the honey and finish with the cinnamon crumble on top.

COMPRESSED OUZO WATERMELON (VE)

Time
10 minutes
(+ overnight pressing)

SERVES 4–6 (AS A LIGHT DESSERT)

⅛ watermelon, cut lengthways into a long triangular wedge
300 ml (10½ fl oz) ouzo

Notes

- To weigh down the watermelon while compressing, I like to use a mortar or a pestle. Use whatever fits on your tray.
- If you don't have time to compress the watermelon overnight, even an hour will be enough to infuse with the ouzo.

Twenty per cent of you will love this and the rest will shudder in disgust, but I am going to need you to hear me out. Traditionally, when it comes to dessert in Greece, often it is just some fresh fruit and ouzo or raki as a digestive to finish a meal. This recipe is a fun play on that. A lot of people swear they don't like ouzo, but I am on a mission to change that. The ouzo is used sparingly and mixed with water, allowing the ouzo to gently penetrate the watermelon overnight, leaving you with a gorgeously perfumed and slightly aniseed flavour that doesn't overpower the fruit.

Leaving the skin on, cut the watermelon into triangular slices about a thumb's width wide. Place them in a deep airtight container lying flat, trying to fit them in as tightly as you can (multiple layers are fine). Pour the ouzo over, then add enough water to just cover the watermelon.

Cover with a sheet of baking paper, then a small tray and a heavy object on top. (This helps to compress the watermelon; see Notes.) Place in the fridge overnight (see Notes).

Serve as a cute little take on fruit for dessert.

LEMON AND MASTIHA SORBET (VE)

Time
40 minutes
(+ 11 hours freezing)

MAKES 12–15 SCOOPS

4 lemons
1 cup (220 g) caster (superfine) sugar
½ cup (105 g) demerara sugar (see Notes)
100 ml (3½ fl oz) mastiha (see Notes)

Notes

- If demerara sugar is hard to source, replace with more caster (superfine) sugar.
- Find mastiha at larger bottle shops or specialty Mediterranean grocers. If unavailable, you can replace it with limoncello.
- Before pouring the mixture into the ice cube trays, you can strain out the lemon zest, but I love the textural notes it offers, so it's up to you.
- If your strongest food processor is a smaller one, just do it in batches and mix everything together at the end. A bullet-style blender, such as a NutriBullet, won't work for this. It needs to be a larger, more open food processor so the mixture has space to move around and break up.

Refreshing and addictive are the only ways to describe my lemon and mastiha sorbet. It came together when I was trying to think of an easy dessert for a dinner party, and I ended up making sgroppino (lemon sorbet topped with prosecco). It was the easiest dessert. Everyone loved it, which was such a reward. The tart brightness makes it a delicious finish to any meal. The addition of mastiha gives it a pine, vanilla and earthy characteristic, which goes really well with lemon. This recipe does need the alcohol, because without it, the sorbet will freeze too hard and you won't get that super smooth sorbet.

Start emptying all your ice cube trays – you'll need about three ice trays. Create some space in the freezer for the trays to sit flat.

Finely grate the zest of the lemons into a small saucepan. Add the sugars, then using your fingers, massage the zest into the sugar to release the oils from the zest. Pour in 400 ml (14 fl oz) water and place over medium–low heat just until the sugar melts and everything comes together (you don't want it to come to a simmer). Take off the heat and transfer the mixture to a heatproof bowl. Place in the fridge for 10 minutes, or until cool to the touch.

While the syrup cools, halve the lemons and squeeze the juice until you have 1 cup (250 ml). Add the lemon juice to a large bowl, along with the mastiha and 1 cup (250 ml) water. Mix together with a spoon.

Once the sugar syrup has cooled, pour the lemon juice mixture over the cooled syrup and mix together with a spoon.

Pour the mixture into the ice cube trays (see Notes). Place the trays in the freezer for at least 10 hours or overnight. (You need the ice cubes super frozen, and because of the alcohol and sugar content this will take longer than normal.)

Take the trays out of the freezer and remove the cubes from the trays. (If it's a little tricky, use a small spoon to help it along.) Blitz in your strongest food processor (see Notes). Blitz on the highest speed as quickly as possible until smooth. Pour the mixture into a larger ice-cream-style container, cover with the lid and place in the freezer again for 1 hour, or until scoopable, but with some resistance.

Serve the sorbet in glasses.

YOGHURT PANNA COTTA AND SPICED STRAWBERRIES

Time
35 minutes
(+ overnight setting)

SERVES 8–10

3 platinum gelatine leaves (60 g/2¼ oz in total)
100 g (3½ oz) honey
1 vanilla bean
1 orange
300 ml (10½ fl oz) thickened (whipping) cream
1 cup (250 ml) full-cream (whole) milk
1 cup (260 g) Greek-style yoghurt

SPICED STRAWBERRIES
½ cup (110 g) caster (superfine) sugar
1 cinnamon stick
3 star anise
250 g (9 oz) fresh strawberries

Panna cottas are a very nineties-core kind of dessert. So in my book, I think that deserves a comeback. But not panna cotta in little moulds that you gently pop out – that's so cumbersome and never looks as good as intended. My version is really easy; the mixture comes together in a pot, then is poured into a deep tray to set overnight before spooning out your desired amount. The Greek-style yoghurt gives it this wonderful tang: creamy with beautiful notes of orange and vanilla through it. Plus, the yoghurt allows the vanilla seeds to spread throughout, as opposed to falling to the bottom. I have paired it with spiced strawberries, but feel free to swap them out for whatever fruit is in season, like fresh figs and honey.

Place the gelatine in a bowl of water to soften while you make the panna cotta mixture.

Weigh the honey into a medium saucepan. Split the vanilla bean and scrape the seeds into the pan. Add the vanilla bean. Using a peeler, cut all the peel off the orange until it's bare. Add the orange peel to the pan (reserving the fruit for the spiced strawberries), along with the cream and milk. Place over low heat. Using a whisk, gently help the sugar melt into the mixture and allow everything to infuse. Once the cream begins to steam (not simmer), take the pan off the heat and pour the mixture into a sieve set over a heatproof bowl.

Working quickly, squeeze out any excess water from the gelatine, then add to the bowl and whisk in until the gelatine melts into the mixture. Add the yoghurt and whisk through until smooth. Pour the mixture into a deep, small to medium baking tray or dish and pop any air bubbles. Cover the surface with plastic wrap (to stop a skin forming). Place in the fridge overnight to set.

While the panna cotta chills, make the spiced strawberries. Place the sugar, cinnamon, star anise and ½ cup (125 ml) water in a small saucepan. Halve the reserved orange and squeeze in the juice of both halves. Bring to a simmer over low heat. Cook for 10 minutes. Hull and quarter the strawberries.

Increase heat to medium, then add the strawberry quarters. Simmer for just 1 minute, then take off the heat. Stir just once to allow the strawberries to wilt gently. (You don't want them to turn to mush.) Once cool, transfer the mixture to a heatproof container and place in the fridge until chilled and thickened.

Once the panna cotta has set, use a large serving spoon to cut into the panna cotta, placing a spoon's worth on each serving plate. Top with some spiced strawberries and enjoy all together.

WATERMELON AND MINT SLUSHY (VE)

Time
20 minutes
(+ overnight steeping/freezing)

SERVES 4–5

¼ large watermelon

MINT SYRUP
1 bunch fresh mint
½ cup (110 g) caster (superfine) sugar

PER COCKTAIL
60 ml (2 fl oz) alcohol of choice (see Notes)
30 ml (1 fl oz) fresh lime juice
2 ice cubes
1 fresh mint sprig, for garnishing

Notes

- Choose your favourite alcohol here; any will work. My preference is a white or dark rum, as it goes really well with tropical flavours. Vodka is a great option for a cleaner drink.
- Store the mint syrup in the fridge for up to 6 months. It's also delicious as a cordial base with soda or drizzled over ice-cream. Or use instead of a simple sugar syrup in rum-based cocktails.
- When ready to blitz, you can double or triple the recipe depending on the size of your blender.

Watermelon and mint just scream summer in Greece, and this slushy tastes just as good in Australia or wherever you're residing. The key is the mint syrup, which allows the slushy to stay a pinkish red colour, as opposed to the weird brown it goes with fresh mint. Prepping this drink is super easy, and you can batch blitz them, so if you've got mates coming over for a daytime party, these will be a dream to hand around.

To make the mint syrup, separate the mint leaves from the stems and set aside. Break the mint stems in half and add to a small saucepan, along with the sugar and ¾ cup (185 ml) water. Bring to a gentle simmer over low heat and cook for 12 minutes. Stir through the mint leaves and simmer for 1 more minute. Take off the heat and cool slightly. Pour the syrup into a sterilised airtight container, cover with the lid and steep in the fridge overnight (for how to sterilise, see Notes page 39).

While the mint syrup is steeping, cut off and discard the watermelon skin so you have just the flesh, then cut the flesh into medium cubes. Transfer the watermelon to a container and place in the freezer overnight to freeze.

The next day, strain the mint syrup, discarding the solids (see Notes).

When ready to blitz the slushies, for each serve (see Notes) place 10 pieces of frozen watermelon and 15 ml (½ fl oz) mint syrup in a high-powdered blender, along with the alcohol of choice, lime juice and ice cubes. Blitz on high, giving it a shake to make sure everything is blended, until a smooth, slushy texture forms. Pour into a glass and top with a mint sprig to serve.

FIG LEAF OLD FASHIONED (VE)

Time
30 minutes
(+ overnight infusing)

SERVES 4

FIG LEAF WHISKEY
5 fresh fig leaves
1 cup (250 ml) whiskey (I use Scotch)

FIG LEAF SYRUP
5 fresh fig leaves
½ cup (110 g) caster (superfine) sugar

PER COCKTAIL
Dash of bitters
Ice cubes
1 small fresh fig leaf, for garnishing

Notes

- Here we infuse the fig leaf whiskey overnight, but if you have the time, steep it for 3 days – you won't need to warm the fig leaf whiskey on the stove, just place the fig leaf pieces and whiskey in the container. After 3 days, strain out the fig leaves.
- The fig leaf syrup goes great as a way to flavour a G&Ts or even fancy up some soda water (club soda).
- When ready to serve, you can multiply the quantities to make up to three drinks at once.
- The whiskey will keep for up to a year and the syrup will keep in the fridge for up to 6 months.

If you live in Melbourne, like me, you'll notice the plethora of fig trees that pop up over the months of summer and into autumn. In my head, they're a free ingredient; the trees just grow so many leaves and they're such a great way to flavour recipes without spending any money. The taste is so nutty, figgy and coconutty that it pairs so well with a smoky scotch. A sophisticated next-level drink to finish your next dinner party.

To make the fig leaf whiskey, cut the fig leaves into small to medium pieces. Place in a small saucepan, along with the whiskey and place over very low heat for 5 minutes. (You want to gently warm and wake up the fig leaves to help infuse the whiskey faster, but not cook off any alcohol.) Take off the heat and pour everything into a sterilised, heatproof and airtight container, reserving the pan (for how to sterilise, see Notes page 39). Cover with the lid and stand at room temperature overnight to infuse (see Notes).

After you've poured the fig leaf whiskey into the container, make the fig leaf syrup. Chop the fig leaves into small to medium pieces and place in the reserved pan, along with the sugar and 1 cup (250 ml) water. Bring to the boil, stirring, until the sugar dissolves. Reduce heat to low and gently simmer for 10 minutes, or until the syrup has a figgy and coconut flavour to it. Take off the heat and pour everything into a sterilised, heatproof and airtight container. Cool slightly, then cover with the lid and place in the fridge overnight to infuse.

The next day, strain the fig leaves out of the syrup and you'll be left with this insanely figgy and nutty syrup (see Notes).

Place coupe cocktail glasses in the freezer to chill while you make the cocktail.

When ready to serve, for each cocktail (see Notes), pour 60 ml (2 fl oz) fig leaf whiskey, 15 ml (½ fl oz) fig leaf syrup and the bitters into a cocktail mixing jug, cocktail shaker or pint glass and fill with ice cubes. Stir with a bar spoon or chopstick for 45 seconds, or until the jug is frosted and it's so cold you can barely touch it. Strain the old fashioned into a chilled glass. Finish with a small fig leaf garnish.

PICKLED PEPPERS (VE)

TOURSI

Time
15 minutes
(+ overnight pickling)

MAKES 1 LARGE JAR

- 6 garlic cloves
- 30 g (1 oz) fresh dill
- 4 dried bay leaves
- 15–20 yellow bullhorn (banana) peppers (see Notes)
- ½ cup (125 ml) white wine vinegar
- ½ cup (125 ml) white vinegar
- ¼ cup (55 g) white (granulated) or caster (superfine) sugar
- 2 tablespoons salt
- 1 tablespoon black peppercorns
- 1 tablespoon coriander seeds

Notes

- I've used bullhorn peppers here as they're easy to source, but you can also use fresh Greek gold peppers or friggitello peppers, if you can find them.
- Leave the peppers whole if you're happy for a longer pickle (they'll be ready in a week) or slice them for a quicker pickle (overnight).
- If your jar won't sit well on its lid, don't worry about flipping it upside down. Just let it cool facing upwards.
- These pickles will keep in the fridge for up to a month, sometimes longer – just look out for any mould or funky smells after the 1-month mark.

Like many older civilisations all over the world, pickling is a big part of Greece's food history. Vegetables such as cucumber, carrots and even cauliflower were steeped in vinegar brines to preserve the produce and allow Greeks to enjoy them well past their seasonal output. My favourite kind of Greek pickle is pickled peppers. Very mild in heat, super punchy on the vinegar acidity and a great addition to a lot of Greek dishes, including the ones in this book. Yellow bullhorn (banana) peppers are used for this, but feel free to use this pickling technique for a range of vegetables; making toursi is so easy and as time goes on, they just get better and better.

Halve the garlic cloves, then place half in a large, sterilised heatproof jar, along with half the dill fronds and bay leaves (for how to sterilise, see Notes page 39). Squish the peppers into the jar so they're nice and tight with little gaps around them. Top with the remaining garlic, dill and bay leaves, pushing into all the crevices so they're spread more evenly.

Place the vinegars, sugar, salt, peppercorns, coriander seeds and 1 cup (250 ml) water in a saucepan over medium–low heat. Bring the pickling liquid almost to a simmer, then as soon as it starts to bubble, pour into the jar, so that the hot liquid hits the peppers, making sure the peppers are completely submerged. Seal with the lid, being careful not to burn yourself and making sure it's secure. Turn the jar upside down to help seal the lid with the heat (see Notes). Cool to room temperature.

Once the jar is cool to the touch, place in the fridge overnight and you can start enjoying the pickles the next day. Store them in the fridge and enjoy as time goes on and they begin to pickle more and more.

CHICKPEA SOUP (VE)

Time
1 hour 30 minutes
(+ 8 hours soaking)

SERVES 6

REVITHIA

375 g (13 oz) dried chickpeas
¼ cup (60 ml) olive oil
1 red onion
2 celery stalks
2 carrots
1 lemon
3 garlic cloves
2 teaspoons dried oregano
2 teaspoons dried rosemary
2 fresh or dried bay leaves
4 cups (1 litre) vegetable stock
1 bunch Tuscan kale (cavolo nero)
1 heaped tablespoon tahini
1 tablespoon plain (all-purpose) flour
Salt, to taste

Hearty vegan soups are such a joy, and this chickpea soup is as traditional Greek as it gets. Revithia takes a bit of time, but the reward is wonderful. It is made with humble ingredients, so you don't need to spend a lot here. Plus, it reheats like a dream. I have added Tuscan kale (cavolo nero) to get greens in there, but feel free to use any leafy greens available to you, such as spinach or silverbeet (Swiss chard). The lemon thickener (a mix of lemon juice, tahini and flour) added near the end makes this soup creamy. You can also thicken it by blitzing some chickpeas from the pot and adding them back in, but the lemon thickener is less effort. The tahini gives it body, while adding a touch of nuttiness. If you like tahini, feel free to go ham and add more than suggested.

Place the chickpeas in a bowl and cover with water. Cover with plastic wrap. Leave at room temperature to soak for a minimum of 8 hours (see Notes).

Heat a large saucepan over low heat, then add the oil. While the pan heats up, roughly dice the onion and celery, adding to the pan as you go. Peel and dice the carrots. Add to the pan, with 1 teaspoon salt. Sauté, stirring, for 5 minutes. (You don't want colour; just enough to break down and become translucent.)

Meanwhile, drain the chickpeas in a colander and rinse them really well.

Finely grate the zest of the lemon into the pan. Finely dice the garlic, then add to the pan, along with the chickpeas and herbs. Increase heat to medium. Stir for 1 minute, then pour in the stock and 1 cup (250 ml) water. Increase heat to high and bring to a simmer. Reduce heat to low so it gently bubbles away, then cover with the lid and simmer for 45 minutes.

While the chickpea mixture is simmering, remove the kale stems and tear the leaves into small to medium pieces. Prep the lemon thickener by halving the lemon and squeezing the juice of both halves into a heatproof bowl. Add the tahini and flour, and mix until a smooth slurry forms.

After 45 minutes of simmering, add the kale to the pan and stir through. Cover and continue to simmer for a further 5 minutes.

Stir a ladle of chickpea mixture into the thickener to temper and make it as smooth as possible. Pour into the pan, stir through, cover with the lid and simmer for a further 10 minutes (so an hour all up). Check the chickpeas – they should be soft, but hold their shape (see Notes).

Season with salt, remove the bay leaves, then serve up hot.

HACK THE RECIPE

Skip the chickpea soaking by using a drained 400 g (14 oz) tin of chickpeas. Shorten the simmering time to your liking. It won't take as long because tinned chickpeas are already cooked and soft.

Notes

- Begin this recipe the night before, or in the morning before work for dinner that night.
- Soaking the chickpeas allows them to absorb the water and helps make them soft enough to cook with.
- After the soup has simmered away for an hour, check if the chickpeas need a bit longer. The time will depend on the freshness of the chickpeas – older ones might need a bit more love on the stove.

TASTES EVEN BETTER THE NEXT DAY

FETA AND KALAMATA MARTINI

Time
10 minutes
(+ overnight infusing)

SERVES 4

FETA-INFUSED GIN
80 g (2¾ oz) feta cheese
1 cup (250 ml) gin (see Notes)

PER COCKTAIL
15 ml (½ fl oz) dry vermouth
15 ml (½ fl oz) kalamata olive brine, strained
Ice cubes
3 kalamata olives, pitted
Extra-virgin olive oil, for garnishing (optional)

HACK THE RECIPE
Skip making the feta gin and just use gin. It will be a dirtier kalamata martini. Add some feta cheese as a garnish to give it some of the same flavour as above.

Notes
- If you prefer a vodka martini, make feta vodka instead of gin.
- When ready to serve, you can multiply the quantities to make up to three drinks at once.
- The feta gin will last up to a year in the fridge, but it's best used within a few months as the flavour starts to drop off. Use in a G&T or instead of ouzo in any of my recipes, like the Fried kefalograviera cheese (page 34).

Now, hear me out. Feta and kalamata olives are actually the perfect addition to a classic martini. The feta is tangy and the olive brine is salty, with that Greek umami that pairs nicely with botanical gin. This drink is sophisticated, modern and you can pass it around with very minimal effort.

To make the feta-infused gin, finely crumble the feta into a sterilised jar (for how to sterilise, see Notes page 39). Pour in the gin, cover with the lid and give the jar a shake. Place in the fridge overnight (or 24 hours for the best results).

The next day, place a coffee filter paper in a sieve and set over a large bowl or jug. Pour the gin through the filter paper and stand until all the gin has dripped through.

Place coupe cocktail glasses in the freezer to chill while you make the cocktail.

When ready to serve, for each cocktail (see Notes), pour 60 ml (2 fl oz) feta-infused gin into a cocktail mixing jug, cocktail shaker or pint glass, along with the vermouth and olive brine. Fill up with ice cubes. Stir with a bar spoon or chopstick for 30–45 seconds, or until the jug is frosted and it's so cold you can barely touch it. Strain the martini into a chilled glass. Skewer the olives onto a cocktail stick and place in the martini. Add 3 drops of oil on top to finish, if using.

ABOUT THE AUTHOR

Conor Curran, one of Australia's most captivating food and beverage creators, brings bold flavours, handcrafted cocktails and his vibrant Greek culture into everything he touches. His upbringing in Clifton Hill, Melbourne, and years spent around his yiayia's table fuelled his love for Greek food and the dream of keeping those recipes alive, one bite at a time.

Starting a career in hospitality in his early teenage years, he followed his love of restaurants into a bachelor's degree in culinary management at William Angliss Institute. From there he worked at renowned restaurants all over Melbourne, including a brief stint in London. When hospitality closed during Covid, he took a shot at applying for MasterChef and went on to become a fan favourite.

Off the back of his television escapades on MasterChef Australia, Conor has established himself as one of the country's leading food and beverage creators. His charm, creativity and culinary intuition have made him a stand-out personality both on and off screen, captivating over 1 million+ people across Instagram and TikTok.

As much as he enjoys cooking, Conor has always preferred eating, making his foray into creating recipes a very delicious and rewarding expedition.

TO MY VILLAGE (THANK YOUS)

'Greek food and the eating of it has always been a collective experience. It really does take a village. This book is no different.

A village is coffee shared without asking, feeding you when you're tired, reminding you who you are when you forget. It's a fig pulled from a tree and torn to share between two, the pouring of ouzo around a table; so joyous is the energy you forget you even had a phone to check.

Time slows to a human pace, measured in greetings, shared meals and stories passed like bread. In that village, you are never only one person; you are part of a small, enduring we.'

First off, none of this would be possible without my Lemonates and Lemon Wedges (my social followers' nickname). Your belief and support from the moment I entered onto your screens back in 2021 has been nothing short of heartwarming. No matter when you joined me during my time on social media, thank you for the likes, the comments, and continuously watching me cook the food I love and shake the cocktails I revere. Creamy Confusion would be nothing without you all, and this book would never have happened.

The dream team that is Max, Lee and Armelle, who helped bring everything that floats around between my ears onto this printed page. Max, my boobelah, thank you for helping me create the recipes so beautifully to be shot, and an even bigger thank you for doing all the dishes. Lee and Mel, I lucked out being paired up with both of you. I still don't know how you made my vision come to life, but just ten times better than I could've ever imagined.

Jemma, you drove me around Melbourne for an entire Sunday helping grab ingredients. You're always there, rain or shine. You're the person I am most excited to hand this book to.

To my chosen family (you all know who you are) that scatter themselves around Australia and the UK, I would not be the person I am today without all of your continued love and pushing me to always try to better myself as a person. I would never have had the confidence to get myself to this position without you all. I will forever be indebted.

Yiayia Maria, my love of Greek food and cooking starts with you. Every single recipe stems from my adolescence sitting on your plastic-covered furniture eating freshly baked bread with kalamata olives and feta, crumbs framing my lips.

To the team at Murdoch Books, there are so many of you who have just championed me from day one, and because of that I am so proud of the book we have created together. This process is not quick, it really is a labour of love. I appreciate the way I have been gently corralled in the right direction, while still allowing my creative mind to roam free.

To Genevieve Day, you took a chance on me years ago when I had a couple of followers and the ruthless desire to do something in food, and I hope I have repaid that faith.

Lastly, to the man who has eaten every single recipe in this cookbook. You watched me for over a year throw everything into *Eat More Greek*, and you happily worked around the madness that was the sink and surrounding areas. When I finished the draft, you proposed, and forever this book will be synonymous with you becoming my fiancé. It makes what was already such a special experience, one that will keep me warm for many years to come.

H

I

J

K

L

Published 2026 by Murdoch Books, an imprint of
Allen & Unwin

MURDOCH BOOKS AUSTRALIA
Cammeraygal Country
83 Alexander Street
Crows Nest NSW 2065
Phone: +61 (0)2 8425 0100
murdochbooks.com.au
info@murdochbooks.com.au

MURDOCH BOOKS UK
Ormond House
26–27 Boswell Street
London WC1N 3JZ
Phone: +44 (0) 20 8785 5995
murdochbooks.co.uk
info@murdochbooks.co.uk

For corporate orders and custom publishing, contact our business development team at salesenquiries@murdochbooks.com.au

Publisher: Melissa Kayser
Editorial manager: Andrea O'Connor
Design manager: Megan Pigott
Designer: Claire Rochford
Editor: Alex McDivitt
Photographer: Armelle Habib
Stylist: Lee Blaylock
Production manager: Natalie Crouch

Murdoch Books acknowledges the Traditional Owners of the Country on which we live and work. We pay our respects to all Aboriginal and Torres Strait Islander Elders, past and present.

Our authorised representative in the EU for product safety is Easy Access System Europe, Mustamäe tee 50, 10621 Tallinn, Estonia, gpsr.requests@easproject.com

ISBN 978 1 76150 134 0

NATIONAL LIBRARY OF AUSTRALIA
A catalogue record for this book is available from the National Library of Australia

A catalogue record for this book is available from the British Library

Colour reproduction by Megan Ellis
Printed in China by 1010 Printing International Limited

OVEN GUIDE: You may find cooking times vary depending on the oven and oven setting you are using. For fan-forced (convection) ovens, as a general rule, set the oven temperature to 20°C (25–50°F) lower than indicated in the recipe.

TABLESPOON MEASURES: We have used 20 ml (4 teaspoon) tablespoon measures. If you are using a 15 ml (3 teaspoon) tablespoon add an extra teaspoon of the ingredient for each tablespoon specified.

10 9 8 7 6 5 4 3 2 1

FSC www.fsc.org MIX Paper | Supporting responsible forestry FSC® C016973